# The Present Reformation of the Church

*Noel Woodroffe*

**EMI Publications**
Miami, Florida &
Trinidad, West Indies

Unless otherwise indicated, all scriptural quotations are from the
*New King James Version* of the Bible.

*The Present Reformation of the Church*
Published by:
EMI Publications
8181 NW 36th St Suite 20H
Miami, FL 33166 &
P.O. Bag 317
Trinidad, West Indies
ISBN 976-8115-03-3

Cover design and book production by:
DB & Associates Design & Distribution
P.O. Box 52756, Tulsa, OK 74152
www.dbassoc.org

Printed in the United States of America.

# Dedication

To my girls Joanna, Nicola and Janelle, and to their generation, the true inheritors of the Present Reformation.

# Contents

# Chapter 1
# Defining the Reformation

At the dawning of a new millenium, the earth has found itself in the midst of the most significant series of changes it has experienced, since the Church was birthed in Jerusalem after the Holy Spirit fell upon the early apostles on the Day of Pentecost. There is a move of God taking place in the earth today. It is not localized to any particular culture or to any ethnic or racial group. It is not limited to any particular economic segment of the world or contained within any preconceived organizational constraints. God is breaking out of traditional boundaries and out of the formerly set paradigms in the global church. A paradigm can be defined as a set mentality that conditions all of our responses and behavior patterns in normal situations of life. God is breaking and transforming those paradigms. He is doing something completely unforeseen, different and new.

You have heard; see all this. And will you not declare it? I have made you hear new things from this time, even hidden things, and you did not know them.

They are created now and not from the beginning; and before this day you have not heard them, lest you should say, 'Of course I knew them.'
Isaiah 48:6,7

The new thing that God is doing in the earth cannot be limited to the term "revival". It is in fact a complete "Reformation of the Church" in all the earth. The word is

1

found in the New Testament in *Hebrews 9:6* in the context of the great structural change from the order of the Old Covenant to that of the New Covenant. We will speak in detail of this change later in this volume as it established principles for spiritual reformation movements of the Lord.

The word "reformation" (*Greek: diorthosis*) means to make a structural adjustment; to make straight again that which is broken, protrudes or has become misaligned or misshapen; to put back into the correct order or form. The meaning points to a skeletal adjustment or to a correction of the inner mechanisms which give shape or form to the outer image. Thus in its application to things spiritual concerning the Church of Jesus Christ it points to a deep, inner structural overhaul of mentality, understanding, behaviors, positions, attitudes and perceptions that provide the inner energy to the outer and visible shape of the Church in the world. God is redesigning in a profound and total way the outer manifestation of the Church in the earth, by means of a deep inner change in all the inner workings of the Body of Christ. We are in the midst of a Reformation of the Church that is much more profound and far-reaching than that which came through the life of Martin Luther in the middle of the sixteenth century.

## Startling the Nations

The profoundly changing manifestation of the Church in the earth will, in the deepest way, affect how the world views or understands Christ and what His significance is to all mankind.

**Listen! Your watchmen lift up their voices; together they shout for joy. When the LORD returns to Zion, they will see it with their own eyes.**

**Burst into songs of joy together, you ruins of Jerusalem, for the LORD has comforted His people, He has redeemed Jerusalem.**

2

> The LORD *will lay bare His holy arm in the sight of all the nations, and all the ends of the earth will see* the salvation of our God.

> Depart, depart, go out from there! Touch no unclean thing! Come out from it and be pure, you who carry the vessels of the LORD.

> But you will not leave in haste or go in flight; for the LORD will go before you, the God of Israel will be your rear guard.

> See, my servant will act wisely; he will be raised and lifted up and highly exalted.

> Just as there were many who were appalled at him — his appearance was so disfigured beyond that of any man and his form marred beyond human likeness —

> *So will he sprinkle many nations, and kings will shut their mouths because of him.* For what they were not told, they will see, and what they have not heard, they will understand.
>
> **Isaiah 52:8-15 (NIV)**

The day of the Lord's visitation is a day of joy in the Church! God's intention is to reveal Himself in a fresh way to the nations of the earth. He will "bare His holy arm in the sight of the nations". This speaks of the strength of the Lord being apprehended by the nations of the earth. This prophetic word operates on two levels. It is on one level a prophecy of Jesus and of His suffering on the cross, but that event did not fully accomplish all of the details of this prophetic word. Jesus in His physical body was not brutalized and disfigured "beyond human likeness" and "more than any other man". In fact crucifixion was a regular punishment meted out by the Romans to criminals and seditionists of the day. Two other individuals were crucified along with Him. Jesus was beaten with thirty-nine lashes but Paul received five times what Jesus received *(2 Corinthians 11:24,25)*.

3

This prophetic word more accurately refers to the distortion of His appearance and the accuracy of His manifestation to the world. The world, because of inaccurate positions of the Church, has seen a distorted presentation of Christ. This reformation move of God will "sprinkle many nations". The word translated "sprinkle" is the Hebrew word *"nazah"*: to startle or to leap in surprise. It speaks of a shocking reality of a new appearance coming to the nations of the earth that causes them to leap in astonishment. Kings, referring to political and rulership systems of the earth, shall *"shut* their *mouths* at (the sight of) Him". The word "shut" can also mean "to spring or to leap" and describes a sudden convulsive action taking place. "Mouth" *peh (Hebrew)* is used in another form in *Proverbs 8:3* to refer to the "doors" of the city. This new revelation or unveiling of Christ in a more accurate way will cause the systems of the earth to convulse in surprise at all of the stronghold entrances to the world system. The Reformation is bringing a new mighty impact upon the nations of the earth.

New revelation will come to the nations on a level they have not formerly received. They will begin to hear what had not been told them before and begin to perceive, with a fresh understanding, what had not been before revealed about the mercy, authority and sovereignty of Christ in the earth.

## Breaking the Seals

Prophet Habakkuk confronted in his day similar conditions in the earth that we confront today:

> **O LORD, how long shall I cry, and You will not hear? Even cry out to You, "Violence!" And You will not save.**

> **Why do You show me iniquity, and cause me to see trouble? For plundering and violence are before me; there is strife, and contention arises.**

> **Therefore the law is powerless, and justice never goes forth.** For the wicked surround the righteous; therefore perverse judgment proceeds
>
> **Habakkuk 1:2-4**

He was crying out for a new move of God in a world in which violence, injustice and contention seemed to be prevailing. Habakkuk desired a spiritual explosion to smite the wickedness of his day. This entire book contains spiritual and prophetic applications to our time. The sworn promise of God *(Numbers 14:21)* is repeated in *Habakkuk 2:14*. The knowledge of the glory of God will fill the earth: this is a prophetic end-time promise of God.

God suddenly responds to the prophet's cry to Him:

> **"Look among the nations and watch — be utterly astounded! For I will work a work in your days which you would not believe, though it were told you.**
>
> **Habakkuk 1:5**

The starting requirement is to possess a global vision; we must be able to "Look among the nations...". Reformation requires an expanded and elevated vision. It demands that we come out of perception limitations and break our vision boundaries. Without a renovated vision we will not perceive what God is doing in the earth today. It is not primarily accessed by personal and individual manifestation but by prophetic perception. A Church that is captured by cultural and ethnic limitations and that is defined by denominational and organizational codes will not have the ability to move into the vast global movement of God in the day of Reformation. It is God that will astound us. To be astounded is to be hit with surprise and wonder as we perceive something taking place that is outside our borders of understanding. Reformation is not controlled by man; it is initiated and supervised by God Himself. It operates outside of our control. Even if God detailed to us what He would do we would still be utterly dumbfounded when He actually does it. Such is the magnitude of the promised move of God in the day of Reformation that Habakkuk saw in our time.

The prophet pursues God for deeper understanding of this end-time event.

> **I will stand my watch and set myself on the rampart, and watch to see what He will say to me, and what I will answer when I am corrected.**
>
> **Habakkuk 2:1**

God's response makes it plain that these awesome events planned for the earth will occur in a divinely appointed time that is designated for a period called "the end". These events which Habakkuk could scarcely understand will be easily accessed in those days and will trigger great activity among the people of God who "read" and understand the vision. There will be no confusion, for the vision will be made "plain" or easily understood and it will communicate its mystery in those days: "it will speak and it will not lie".

> **Then the LORD answered me and said: "Write the vision and make it plain on tablets, that he may run who reads it.**
>
> **For the vision is yet for an appointed time; but at the end it will speak, and it will not lie. Though it tarries, wait for it; because it will surely come, it will not tarry.**
>
> **Habakkuk 2:2,3**

The main key is that those things which the ancient prophets could not understand, would be easily accessed by those who "read" the vision in the end-time. That which was shrouded in mystery would be no longer mysterious. The activity of the prophetic saints of the end would be based upon accurate understanding of that which has been locked up from the understanding of the ancient prophets, but which is made plain at the appointed hour in the latter day. Accurate Kingdom activity in this day of apostolic and prophetic understanding is based on access to fresh revelation of that which is being released by God in the immediate present. Those bound by traditional mentalities and who have rejected present truth prophetic positions will not be able to "run".

In other words God is breaking the seals off the Word in the day of Reformation. In Daniel Chapter 12, the prophet is given knowledge of the awesome events of the end-time in the earth. Although he clearly hears the words spoken to him yet he cannot understand what he is actually hearing. The meaning of the words is locked from his prophetic understanding *(Daniel 12:8)*. He is commanded to "shut up the words and *seal* the book *until* the time of the end" *(Daniel 12:4)*.

It is important to notice that it is not God who seals the book, it is Daniel who is commanded to shut up and seal the book. It is prophetic impartation and frequency that seals the book; it will take prophetic impartation and frequency to access it when the time comes in a day of increased Kingdom activity and increase of knowledge. This is a clear description of our time. There are conditions indicated which define the season when at last the seals will be broken and the saints have prophetic access to the technology of the events of the end:

> **Many shall be purified, made white, and refined, but the wicked shall do wickedly; and none of the wicked shall understand, but the wise shall understand.**
>
> **Daniel 12:10**

It is a day of purification and refining of Kingdom positions in the earth. This purification will cause a fresh offering to be made to the Lord *(Malachi 3:2)*. Many ministries across the earth will be purified and renovated to

make them able to stand in this time of Reformation.
There will be an increasingly clear contrast between
what is of God and what is not; "the wicked will do
wickedly". The prophecy defines conditions in the earth
which are demarcated by the level and power of understanding that we possess. The wicked will be totally
ignorant, but the "wise" (or those who live in the power
of unsealed prophetic understanding) will have access
to understanding of that which even Daniel could not
comprehend in his day.

## The Apostolic Core of Reformation

At the very core of this present Reformation move
of God in the earth today is the current release of revelation, understanding and function of apostolic operations in the Church and in the wider Kingdom of God.
I strongly advise that you read my book *Uncovering
Apostolic Technology* for a deeper understanding of the
many dimensions of the apostolic ministry today. The
Apostolic Move of God brings not only a release of apostles to the Body of Christ, but more importantly a powerful release of apostolic impartation and the ministering
of an apostolic spirit and mentality to the entire Body of
Christ. This apostolic impartation is the resource that
gives momentum and breakthrough power for the next
phase of God's Reformation movings in the earth.

God Himself has given precedence to the apostolic
in the Church:

> And God has appointed these in the church: *first
> apostles,* second prophets, third teachers, after that mir-
> acles, then gifts of healings, helps, administrations,
> varieties of tongues.
>
> 1 Corinthians 12:28

First is the Greek word *"proton"*: *first in time, place,
influence, rank and order.* The word "first" does not indicate that apostles are better than any other ministry and
must rule over them. All five giftings represent different

dimensions of the Christ anointing and all have come from God. There is no dimension of Christ that is superior or inferior to any other. That is theologically and practically impossible. Christ is perfection and contains no lesser or more defective parts as compared to any other.

The word "first" indicates a peculiar quality of the apostolic gift. It has breakthrough capability that may not be manifested as powerfully in other giftings. Whenever God is moving into new territory in a fresh Reformation move to radically restructure the Church and the world, He releases the "first" anointing of the apostolic or the breakthrough potential of the apostolic anointing. Martin Luther was an apostle who tore open the walls of the medieval Roman Catholic church and caused fresh manna to come to the Church in his day of Reformation.

Ranking for function does not necessarily mean that "first" is qualitatively better. God is a Trinity — three Persons in One God. The Holy Spirit is as much God as is Jesus or God the Father, yet every Christian understands that there is a functional headship in the Trinity. Father is the functional head yet is equal in power and divinity to Christ or the Holy Spirit *(1 Corinthians 11:3).*

Apostles provide a functional headship to the Church because they possess a building, governmental anointing designed to give the Church penetration, breakthrough, clarity in the design of God and an order in which the power of God can move unhindered by religious-political clutter. The apostolic release is the arrowhead to the Reformation move of God today.

## The Power of Apostolic Transitions

The apostolic ministry is inseparable from the other governmental ministries given in *Ephesians 4:11.* All are needed to accomplish the work of God and are designed to work as a coherent package. The apostolic is committed to a fully performing and successfully operating Church. The great book of the early Church is called *The Book of the Acts of the Apostles*, but in it we see a fully functioning Church in which every governmental ministry and all the saints are operational and powerful.

This apostolic-led Reformation move of God gains its power and authority as it operates out of a clear sense of the value of the past. It affirms the doings of God in the past, but it is committed to bringing *the entire Church* into a migration towards an accurate and God-embraced future. The clear sense and appreciation of a season of transition is very vital to efffective release of Reformation.

In *2 Samuel 1:17-27* David leads Israel into a very powerful season of transition. Saul and his sons are dead; the old order of government in Israel has passed away and now a new season is about to begin. This new Davidic order will re-activate all the covenant promises of God and ultimately bring forth the powerful temple-building order of Solomon which will bring a manifest demonstration of the glory of God to the earth in the glorious temple. David teaches Israel *The Song of the Bow* in which he honors the accomplishments of Saul and Jonathan and leads the people into and past the grief of a fallen order towards a place of new enquiry for the fresh directions of the Lord.

> **It happened after this that David inquired of the LORD, saying, "Shall I go up to any of the cities of Judah?" And the LORD said to him, "Go up." David said, "Where shall I go up?" And He said, "To Hebron."**
>
> **2 Samuel 2:1**

Reformation goes beyond the grief for that which is past and into fresh enquiry of God for a relevant direction for powerful advance. *The Song of the Bow* is the technology of spiritual transition and must be taught to the people of transition by the leaders of the new order of Reformation.

The Book of Nehemiah ends with a powerful move towards Reformation as the people bind themselves in the signing of a new agreement with God that involved not only a change of heart attitude but also included new systems of taxation to support the activities of the house of God, new revised dwelling patterns in Jerusalem and in the surrounding cities, revised duties of the priests and Levites and new commercial regulations for trade and merchandise in the city of Jerusalem *(Nehemiah 9:39;10:28-29)*. But this document of Reformation is activated only after the people come to a clear understanding of their journey to that point through an examination of their history. The great prayer of the Levites takes the people on a journey through their historical relationship with God. They not only come to a clear prophetic understanding of their journey, but also they at last begin to discern the true intent of the heart of God to bring a people to Himself *(Nehemiah 9:5-38)*.

After this pattern, every great Reformation must bring people to a place of deep understanding. Without understanding people will not change their position. They will see change as inflicted pain and not perceive the prophetic necessity to embrace change in order to bring to fulfillment the deep purposes of God. When the heart of a people is changed under the dynamic apostolic impartation of a season of Reformation, they begin to see in the changes taking place in their spiritual environment, the fulfillment of their heart's desire. They will come to a place of acceptance and willingness and cease to fight against God and reject that which is fresh and new:

**"When leaders lead in Israel, when the people willingly offer themselves, bless the LORD!"**

**Judges 5:2**

11

> The LORD shall send the rod of Your strength out
> of Zion. Rule in the midst of Your enemies!
>
> Your *people shall be volunteers in the day of Your*
> *power;* in the beauties of holiness, from the womb of
> the morning, you have the dew of Your youth.

> **Psalm 110:2,3**

A true dynamic reformation cannot be imposed upon the minds of people. The saints must be led into a new experience which they themselves embrace as a vital necessity for progression in the spiritual journey towards completion of the will of God. In Nehemiah's Reformation, it was those who had knowledge and understanding that went forward to the stage of new covenant *(Nehemiah 10:28)*. They were not coerced, but willingly "made for ourselves" *(Nehemiah 10:32)* the ordinances that exacted from themselves the fresh mandate for Kingdom activity.

## Chapter 2
# Foundations for the
# Present Reformation

We must remember that when God moves in the earth He does not give a name to His moving. Men apply names to the spiritual movements of God in order to provide clarity and definition; however names can sometimes lock in the minds of men to perceive only very narrow areas of manifestation, while God may be moving along a fairly broad bandwidth and doing several things across the globe all at the same time. We must be careful that our definitions are therefore flexible and not binding and dogmatic. We must provide clear and precise descriptions of what God is doing, while not creating walls and new strongholds in the minds of men that make it difficult for future migration to new levels of understanding in the continuing prophetic activities of God in the earth.

Several names have been used to describe our perceptions of what God is now doing in the earth such as:

*The Post-Denominational Move of God*

*The Second Reformation*

*The Apostolic/Prophetic Move of God*

*The Global Prayer Movement*

*The Apostolic Reformation*

All of these names point to either several or single dimensions of the total moving of God in the earth that are identifiable at the present time and all are accurate definitions of aspects of His moving.

Let us briefly list some easily observable features of this present move that can be identified across the globe in every sector of the Church, that will help us into a general comprehension of the Present Reformation of the Church.

• *A complete radical renovation of the mentality of the Church as God removes all aspects of limitation from our faith.*

God, by His Spirit, through the power of apostolic impartation, is moving the global Church to inhabit an entirely new paradigm for the 21$^{st}$ century. The strength of apostolic warfare is in the breaking of fossilised, religious mentalities behind which Pharisee spirits have taken up strong residence in the Church preventing effective advance of the Kingdom.

> For the weapons of our (apostolic) warfare are not carnal but mighty in God for pulling down strongholds.
>
> Casting down arguments and every high thing that exalts itself against the knowledge of God, bringing every thought into captivity to the obedience of Christ,
>
> And being ready to punish all disobedience when your obedience is fulfilled.
>
> 2 Corinthians 10:4-6
>
> "But woe to you, scribes and Pharisees, hypocrites! For you shut up the kingdom of heaven against men; for you neither go in yourselves, nor do you allow those who are entering to go in."
>
> Matthew 23:13

It is only through renovation of old mentalities that we can access the progressive nature of the will of God for our time:

> Do not conform any longer to the pattern of this world, but *be transformed by the renewing of your mind.* Then you will be able to test and approve what God's will is — his good, pleasing and perfect will.
>
> Romans12:2 (NIV)

• *A recognition that we are a generation of destiny, coming rapidly into the realisation that we are in the best position to actually bring an end to the ages in our time.*

This is the first time in the history of the Church since the early days of the book of Acts that there has been released among us a general understanding and acceptance of apostolic and prophetic ministry as valid and teachable functions of the Spirit in the Body of Christ. For centuries we have "killed the prophets and stoned those who were sent (apostles)" (Matthew 23:37). Now that these ministries have again been received and the full five-fold dimension of Christ is operational in the Body of Christ we are prepared for the massive thrust toward the actual completion of the purposes of Christ in the earth. The "set time" of the Lord's favor on the Church has come and the final assault upon the last enemy "death" has begun. There is a prophetic generation that will be released from death:

> You will arise and have mercy on Zion; for the time to favor her, yes, *the set time, has come..*

> For the LORD shall build up Zion. He shall appear in His glory.

> This will be *written for the generation to come, that a people yet to be created* may praise the LORD.

For He looked down from the height of His sanctuary; from heaven the LORD viewed the earth

*...to release those appointed to death,*

To declare the name of the LORD in Zion, and His praise in Jerusalem,

**Psalm 102:14,16,18,19-21**

• *A radical movement away from dead religious tradition and local church limitation to a Kingdom reality that invades every aspect of life.*

A mature Davidic mentality is rising upon the global Church. All restrictions in every realm: social, cultural, political, economic, ethnic, organizational, denominational etcetera, that divide the Body of Christ and hinder the effective advance of the Kingdom, are being shattered by the fire of prophetic and apostolic presence in the Church. The heart-cry of the 21$^{st}$ century Church is for the global expression of the glory of a risen Christ; nothing will stop it!

For by You I can run against a troop; by my God I can leap over a wall.

**2 Samuel 22:30**

The emphasis of the emerging Church is for Kingdom reality. The 21$^{st}$ century believers will not be separated by walls of denomination or ministry ambitions. In this Reformation God is implanting in the hearts of His children the desire to be truly one with each other, to express a global warfare against the domain of darkness:

One runner will run to meet another, and one messenger to meet another, to show the king of Babylon that his city is taken on all sides;

The passages are blocked, the reeds they have burned with fire, and the men of war are terrified.

**Jeremiah 51:31,32**

16

• *A positive bringing in of the mass of ordinary believers into the reality of ministry thus radically broadening the base of the assault upon satanic positions in every area of life.*

God is imparting an apostolic spirit upon the lives of all millenium believers. The purpose of the five governmental ministries has always been not to exalt themselves, but to impart to and equip the saints for effective ministry. In Luke Chapter 10, Jesus equips and sends out seventy believers in a strategic spiritual attack upon the entire region. He sends them "two by two...into every city and place where He Himself was about to go" (Luke 10:1).

These seventy are sent out under the same mandate as the twelve apostles who went out before them (compare Luke 10 with Matthew 10) *but themselves are not apostles.* The seventy represent the fullness of the apostolic spirit for effective breakthrough imparted to the Body of Christ. These seventy break into demonic positions all across the territory and return to Jesus with triumphant news of satanic submissions. Jesus rejoices at their return and at their acquisition of mystery which has been hidden from the wise of ancient time, but is now released to "babes" going out in the power of an apostolic spirit (Luke 10:17-24).

All of the great patriarchal leaders sought to bring the saints in to a greater sense of involvement and empowerment. In Numbers Chapter 11, Moses is releasing a dimension of his spirit upon seventy elders of the Jews. Two of them remain in the camp, but the Spirit comes upon them anyway. In response to the protest of the still youthful Joshua, Moses reveals the heart of any true leader of a Reformation movement among the people of God:

Then Moses said to him, "Are you zealous for my sake? *Oh, that all the LORD'S people were prophets and that the LORD would put His Spirit upon them!"*

Numbers 11:29

• *A complete restructuring of the way the Kingdom is financed and the emergence of faith for huge financial input into the Kingdom for the push to the end of all things.*

This Reformation is bringing forth a prophetic corps of millenium believers designed by the Spirit in their Kingdom mentality to cause great prophetic pronouncements to come to pass in our day. Isaiah prophesied a generation of rising light and brightness; a generation that develops to spiritual power in the midst of the darkening tide of evil in their day. It is to their light that the nations come bringing their wealth for Kingdom advance:

*Arise, shine;* for your light has come! And the glory of the LORD is risen upon you.

For behold, the darkness shall cover the earth, and deep darkness the people; but *the LORD will arise over you, and His glory will be seen upon you.*

*The Gentiles (nations) shall come to your light, and kings to the brightness of your rising.*

"Lift up your eyes all around, and see: they all gather together, they come to you; your sons shall come from afar, and your daughters shall be nursed at your side."

Then you shall see and become radiant, and your heart shall swell with joy; because the abundance of the sea shall be turned to you, *the wealth of the Gentiles (nations) shall come to you.*

Isaiah 60:1-5

• *A ferocious thrust into governmental prayer across the nations of the earth as a tidal wave of prayer and expectation sweeps through demonic territories worldwide.*

I strongly recommend that you read my publication *Governmental Prayer: The Warfare Expression of the Apostolic*, which deals extensively with all of the issues concerning what I call governmental prayer.

The heart of governmental prayer is the issuing of apostolic decrees and prophetic declarations in accordance with the will of God, which blast the purposes of God deep into territory held by ancient demonic positions. Governmental prayer represents the changing spiritual character of the Church into a more glorious, more spiritually militant position against the domain of darkness:

> For Zion's sake I will not hold My peace, and for Jerusalem's sake I will not rest, until her righteousness goes forth as brightness, and her salvation as a lamp that burns.
>
> The Gentiles (nations) shall see your righteousness, and all kings your glory. You shall *be called by a new name,* which *the mouth of the LORD will name.*
>
> You shall also be a crown of glory in the hand of the LORD, and a royal diadem in the hand of your God.
>
> Isaiah 62:1-3

The global Church is indeed being "called by a new name", as its character and spiritual patterns are being revised away from dead religion into the more urgent patterns of biblical accuracy. The mouth of the Lord has consistently throughout scripture referred to the utterance of the prophets *(2 Chronicles 36:12; Jeremiah 9:12; Jeremiah 23:16).* It is the prophetic declaration that is re-modeling the character of the Church towards more glorious patterns, causing advance in the nations.

In Ezra, a book of building of the house of God, representing apostolic technology for the spiritual building of the completed Church of Jesus Christ, the central issues concern the struggle of decree against decree. Both the people of God and the satanic opposition issue powerful decrees that affect the progress of the work of building. The core question that must be settled is "Who commanded you to build..." *(Ezra 5:9)*. In the day of Reformation or the day of effective apostolic building, the issuing of strong decrees in prayer is of prime importance:

> **In the day when your walls are to be built, in that day the decree shall go far and wide.**
>
> **Micah 7:11**

• *A purification of ministry and ministers as new leadership is shifted into place by the Lord, as a global reshuffling of leadership is underway in the Church.*

The Reformation is not limited to one country or one culture. God is changing the former patterns of the Body of Christ. He is calling forth leaders and spokesmen from every corner of the earth and from every society and culture with a strong, authoritative declaration of the "now" purposes of the Lord. In many parts of the earth and in many sectors of the Church, God will require new attitudes of humility as their oligarchic mentalities of spiritual control will be shattered by emergences from different places. In other places God will require mendicant mentalities and depressed levels of personal significance to be broken, as the Spirit demands that leaders come forth into glorious anointings from low places. The Word of the Lord will cover the earth!

but truly, as I live, all the earth shall be filled with the glory of the LORD.

Numbers 14:21

For the earth will be filled with the knowledge of the glory of the LORD, as the waters cover the sea.

Habakkuk 2:14

In the oceans the waters do not pile up in one place. There may be different depths in different places but the waters evenly cover the sea; so too it will be with the glory of the Lord. In this Reformation, God is causing **"apostolic equalization"** to occur in the earth. The word of revelation will not pile up in any one city or one society, but will spread into every culture and every country. Apostolic leaders will rise up from every place with mighty signs and declarations. Such ministry will be purified by the refining fire of the Lord as He suddenly comes to His temple (Church) in the day of Reformation and purges the sons of Levi as gold or silver is purged *(Malachi 3:1-5)*.

• *A global release and acceptance of prophets and apostles, completing and redefining the function and power of the complete package of five-fold governmental ministry.*

For the first time since the book of Acts church, we have operating in the earth the complete package of five ministries as revealed by Paul in *Ephesians 4:11*. These ministries, as separate components brought together, represent the full spectrum of Christ's anointing in the Church today, as they download or impart their resources into the eager, waiting Church. Without the operation of all five governmental ministries the fullness of the awesome array of Christ's power flowing through the Church cannot be seen in the earth.

> **And He Himself gave some to be apostles, some prophets, some evangelists, and some pastors and teachers,**
>
> **for the equipping of the saints for the work of ministry, for the edifying of the body of Christ,**
>
> **till we all come to the unity of the faith and of the knowledge of the Son of God, to a perfect man, *to the measure of the stature of the fullness of Christ;***
>
> **Ephesians 4:11-13**

The effective functioning and interplay of these five ministries will create a strong dynamic in the Body of Christ that will thrust it toward completion of the purposes of God. As the ministries relate to each other and flow as one stream in the purposes of God, they will sharpen and refine each other to hitherto unprecedented levels of power and accuracy.

Much of the spiritual interplay will be a hidden technology, out of sight of open manifestation and natural understanding. It will however be seen in the dramatic increase of the momentum of the global Church, in its thrust towards covenant joinings throughout the Body, and in the shattering of false religious divisions as the Body moves towards the "unity of the faith".

The Church will demonstrate increased ability to bring forth with unhindered strength the final purposes of the Lord, and a powerful end-time warfare that completely dominates and neutralizes the ability of the satanic forces to resist its advance.

As the Reformation matures in the earth and as the Church moves forcefully into the 21st century, competition between the ministry gifts will decrease until it no longer is a factor to be considered. The apostolic ministry will be fully released to take its place at the helm of the advance and the apostles of the future will function in awesome displays of supernatural power and revelation in the earth. They will lead the Church in the last great charge upon the last enemy-death.

> Then comes the end, when He delivers the kingdom to God the Father, when He puts an end to all rule and all authority and power.
>
> For He must reign till He has put all enemies under His feet.
>
> The last enemy that will be destroyed is death.
>
> 1 Corinthians 15:24-26

• *A deliberate, strategised and heightened warfare against all illegitimate spiritual thrones worldwide as the Church presses in for the global harvest of souls for the Kingdom as God closes the ages down.*

The last command of Jesus was an apostolic mandate to disciple and teach the nations:

> And Jesus came and spoke to them, saying, "All authority has been given to Me in heaven and on earth.
>
> Go therefore and make disciples of all the nations, baptizing them in the name of the Father and of the Son and of the Holy Spirit,
>
> teaching them to observe all things that I have commanded you; and lo, I am with you always, even to the end of the age." Amen.
>
> Matthew 28:18-20

The Church has always had a primary responsibility not to be limited to a parish, but to be custodians of the future mentalities and destiny of the entire earth. Jesus has never withdrawn His promised presence in the work "even to the end of the age". The inner vision of Reformation is a vision of lost multitudes groaning for redemption. The thrust of Reformation is to send out workers armed with apostolic mentalities into the harvest of the earth.

But when He saw the multitudes, He was moved with compassion for them, because they were weary and scattered, like sheep having no shepherd.

Then He said to His disciples, "The harvest truly is plentiful, but the laborers are few.

"Therefore pray the Lord of the harvest to *send out laborers into His harvest.*"

And when He had called His twelve disciples to Him, He gave them power over unclean spirits, to cast them out, and to heal all kinds of sickness and all kinds of disease.

*Now the names of the twelve apostles* are these....

Matthew 9:36-38;10:1,2

Reformation is a maturing and developing process. God releases His divine purposes according to His times and seasons determined before the foundation of the earth. His ministers in the Church hear the command from heaven and begin to declare the current position of the Spirit in the earth. Those whose hearts are hungry for God and whose ears are tuned to the frequencies of heaven, hear the voice of the Lord through His prophets and apostles, and begin the awesome process of transformation to fulfil the purpose of the Lord in their lives; and so the journey to the next level begins.

## • *Emphasis upon the internal issues of the faith.*

that I *may know Him* and the power of His resurrection, and the fellowship of His sufferings, being conformed to His death,

if, by any means, I may attain to the resurrection from the dead.

24

Not that I have already attained, or am already per-
fected; but I press on, that I may lay hold of that for
which Christ Jesus has also laid hold of me.

Brethren, I do not count myself to have apprehended; but one thing I do, forgetting those things
which are behind and reaching forward to those things
which are ahead,

*I press toward the goal* for the prize of the upward
call of God in Christ Jesus.

Therefore let us, as many as are mature, have this
mind; and if in anything you think otherwise, God
will reveal even this to you.

Philippians 3:10-15

The renewal of the internal struggle to perfection is
a part of every genuine Reformation move of God. The
cry of the Reformation is to be more like Him as we
return forcefully to the experience of the inner journey,
as an integral part of the salvation process.

The progression of the children of Israel across the
geographical wilderness after they were released by the
powerful Reformation move of Moses, was matched by
an equally powerful journey from ignorance to understanding. It was a journey to accountability, responsibility and maturity. They progressed from a state of weakness to one of battle-ready strength; from a disorderly
rabble oppressed with a mentality of servitude, to an
orderly society that could invade heavily fortified territories and subdue them.

Aged heroes of the faith like Caleb were once abject
slaves in Egypt. Aaron, clad in the rich robes of the High
Priest and lifting up potent sacrifices to God, was once
treading out straw to make bricks in Goshen. This
dynamic and honorable change is also a factor of the
Reformation.

Throughout the Bible there is the drama and the ceremony of drawing closer to God. There is always great grandeur, the lighting of lamps, the lifting of sacrifices, the chants of the congregation in the passage of solemn assemblies. The air is filled with the sounds of the horns and trumpets and with the scent of incense rising up into the nostrils of God.

The physical ceremony and grandeur of the Bible portrays a reality in the heart of God. These things provide prophetic pictures and pointers to the desire of God to see that ceremony and grandeur expressed spiritually in the heart of man. The writer of Hebrews speaks of the majestic grandeur of God's descent upon Sinai, but points us to an even more awesome dimension of majesty, in our present approach to the true things of the Spirit:

> **For you have not come to the mountain that may be touched and that burned with fire, and to blackness and darkness and tempest,**
>
> **and the sound of a trumpet and the voice of words, so that those who heard it begged that the word should not be spoken to them anymore.**
>
> **But *you have come to Mount Zion* and to the city of the living God, the heavenly Jerusalem, to an innumerable company of angels,**
>
> **to the general assembly and church of the firstborn who are registered in heaven, to God the Judge of all, to the spirits of just men made perfect,**
>
> **to Jesus the Mediator of the new covenant, and to the blood of sprinkling that speaks better things than that of Abel.**
>
> **Hebrews 12:18,19,22-24**

Reformation comes to lift us out of spiritual dimensions that have become mundane and to return us to the dimensions where prophets of old fell on their faces before God.

## • *The Globalization of the Church*

Reformation pushes the Church out of its "parish" mentality and towards a more global context. The finalization of the purposes of God absolutely require a Church that has the capacity to effectively impact the earth on a planetary level. Mentality expansion is a necessary ingredient for Reformation.

God's ultimate intent is a move of the Kingdom that assaults the demonic positions globally. The stone in Daniel's vision crushes all of the false mentalities and positions of the demonic domains and consumes them:

> **And in the days of these kings the God of heaven will set up a kingdom which shall never be destroyed; and the kingdom shall not be left to other people; it shall break in pieces and consume all these kingdoms, and it shall stand forever.**
>
> **Daniel 2:44**

Reformation is "the set time" of the Lord's favor on the Church. It is a season of the building up of Zion so that all nations shall fear the Lord:

> **You will arise and have mercy on Zion; for the time to favor her, yes, *the set time, has come.***
>
> **For Your servants take pleasure in her stones, and show favor to her dust.**
>
> **So the nations shall fear the name of the LORD, and all the kings of the earth Your glory.**
>
> **For the LORD shall build up Zion; he shall appear in His glory.**
>
> **Psalm 102:13-16**

The inner sorrow of the move to Reformation produces the upward thrust in God that lifts the Church to a place of fame and acclaim in the nations of the earth:

**"I will gather those who sorrow over the appointed assembly, who are among you, to whom its reproach is a burden.**

**...I will appoint them for praise and fame in every land where they were put to shame."**

**Zephaniah 3:18,19**

My prayer is that as we look into the depths of the Reformation process in the earth today, that your hearts will be deeply stirred and you will be propelled towards the furthest boundaries of Kingdom lifestyle for the believers of the next millenium.

## Chapter 3
# Reformation Spirit and Mentality: Patterns in John the Baptist

## Reformation: The Concept

Reformation occurs where a people make a conscious decision to change the predictable outcomes of their future. Under normal conditions, the present is a direct product of the combination of circumstances and events that have been experienced in the past, and forms the platform for creation of future reality and experience. Whenever a people, looking forward into the future, come to a prophetic realization that their future is no longer accurate and capable of fulfilling the new demands of the purposes of God, then a new future has to be designed by breaking with the patterns of the traditional present. This requires powerful transition to new mentalities, new expectations and faith levels, new revelation from the Word of God for more powerful performance of the purposes of God in the earth. This powerful transition is a Reformation.

Reformation requires the conscious choosing of a preferred destination; it does not occur automatically. Reformation does not overtake the unaware or the unperceptive; it requires obedience, courage and understanding. A Reformation move of God is ordained in heaven and received by prophetic people in the earth, but must be built by activities of sacrifice, joy and persistent proclamation.

"Thus says the LORD of hosts: 'Let your hands be strong, you who have been hearing in these days these words by the mouth of the prophets, who spoke in the day the foundation was laid for the house of the LORD of hosts, *that the temple might be built.*

Zechariah 8:9

Reformation comes to the earth through the pathway of persecution, resistance and extreme hindrances from Pharisee positions established within the Body of Christ itself. Such positions are established by the enemy to block up the advance of the Kingdom in the hearts and minds of men. They will not allow you to enter nor will they enter themselves *(Matthew 23:13).*

## John the Baptist: A Reformation Principle

John the Baptist represents the actualization point of perhaps the greatest and most far-reaching Reformation that has ever occurred in the earth shift from the structural order of Law to the effective spiritual order of Divine Grace. Jesus is about to appear on the earth and He will change everything forever. Life will never again be the same: permanent changes are about to be made.

God is about to bring the entire complex Mosaic system to termination. All of the spiritual technology of heaven will change after John. Priesthoods, sacrifices, cleansings, structures, regulations, traditions and complete sets of historical understandings, which have been given by God to a people for nearly two thousand years will instantaneously become invalid. God will no longer appear in a temple made with hands; He will now be seeking to invest Himself in temples of the heart deep inside the inner life of men.

A great demand for repentance and for shifting of earthly mentalities is issued from heaven, in a way that no prophet who ever lived has ever spoken it into the earth. The prophetic frequencies of John the Baptist have never been heard here on this planet before, and the hearts and minds of men struggle to comprehend this new personality, the new message and the new demand of God. It is a season of Reformation.

John is the effective transition. He is the end of the old and the beginning of the new. He is the announcer of the dawn of a new day for the human race. He comes to shake the mentalities of the past from the moorings of outdated thinking patterns and to introduce the way for things that are new. These are the important characteristics of John. He is both a breaker and a builder. He dresses like Elijah but he speaks of Christ; he shatters earthly religious kingdoms but he establishes a more permanent spiritual Kingdom in the earth. He offers no room for deceptive maneuvering, demanding that every sector of society respond to his message. He is full of urgency because he is the precursor and proclaimer of events that have already been set in motion and have already been birthed into the earth. While John spoke, Jesus was already here, matured but not yet activated by baptism in the Jordan. John was racing against God's irresistible time clock; events would overtake him; the power of God was moving into the earth!

# The John Pattern
# for Reformation Mentality

Let us look into the life and experience of John to find patterns that God placed in the great Reformation of transition from the Old Covenant to the New. In so doing we will rediscover truth that will be applied to our season of Reformation, enabling us to make accurate transition to the new things of the 21$^{st}$ century Church.

> • *The release of an entirely new dimension of ministry and a break with the traditions of the old.*

So it was, on the eighth day, that they came to circumcise the child; and *they would have called him by the name of his father, Zacharias.*

His mother answered and said, *"No; he shall be called John."*

But they said to her, *"There is no one* among your relatives who is called by this name."

So they made signs to his father — what he would have him called.

And he asked for a writing tablet, and wrote, saying, "His name is John." So they all marveled.

*Immediately his mouth was opened and his tongue loosed,* and he spoke, praising God.

Then fear came on all who dwelt around them; and all these sayings were discussed throughout all the hill country of Judea.

And all those who heard them kept them in their hearts, saying, "What kind of child will this be?" And the hand of the Lord was with him.

Now *his father Zacharias was filled with the Holy Spirit, and prophesied,* saying:
Luke 1:59-67

John is a prophetically introduced order that broke with the naming traditions of the traditional family past. The assembled family want to call him by the name of his mute father but this is not to be so. There is no one among his relatives who is called by that strange new name — John, a name in fact given by the messenger from heaven *(Luke 1:13).* It causes all the relatives present to marvel. So too are the patterns of each Reformation move of God. It is named from heaven and at its appearance its identity seems to be not of the traditional order of the Church. Its names, vocabulary, terminology and spiritual patterns seem to be strange to all the hearers, but its new identity has been given by God.

As with Zacharias's experience at the naming of John, so in each Reformation move of God, if the fathers who have become mute and ineffective in the prophetic proclamation of the new thing coming into the earth, accept and receive the new identity from heaven and speak its new name into the earth, they will receive utterance, prophetic power and a fresh activation to new levels of ministry.

God's intention in the day of Reformation is not to destroy and sideline the fathers who have piloted the past moves of God. His desire is to "refire not to retire" them. Part of the awesome technology of the "unity of the faith" *(Ephesians 4:13)* is that we must recover the spiritual technology of the partnership of the spiritual generations. David invested his own substance and that of his people for the future success of Solomon, his son *(1 Chronicles 28:9-21;1 Chronicles 29:1-9).* King David enthroned Solomon even while he was still alive and utters one of the most profound statements of kingship and spiritual leadership in the entire Bible:

> **"'Praise be to the LORD, the God of Israel, who has allowed my eyes to see a successor on my throne today.'"**
>
> **1 Kings 1:48 (NIV)**

• *Reformation points the way to a greater order.*

**In those days John the Baptist came preaching in the wilderness of Judea,**

and saying, "Repent, for the kingdom of heaven is at hand!"

For this is he who was spoken of by the prophet Isaiah, saying: "The voice of one crying in the wilderness: 'Prepare the way of the Lord; make His paths straight.'"

Matthew 3:1-3

"I indeed baptize you with water unto repentance, *but He who is coming after me is mightier than I,* whose sandals I am not worthy to carry. He will baptize you with the Holy Spirit and fire."

Matthew 3:11

The message of John is the message of the Kingdom. Apostle Rinaldo Texidor of Voz en el Desierto Network (the Latin American expression of the World Breakthrough Network) says it this way: "The message of the Kingdom is the gospel of the 21$^{st}$ century." The core emphasis for access to the new things to come, John says, is repentance. The word used is *metanoeo* derived from the words *meta: after* and *noeo: to think.* It identifies a mental exercise that involves a definite change of thinking that terminates in changed activity and behaviour. It is not the result of an emotional, esoteric or mystical experience. It involves the faculties of understanding, the will and definite action. It is the structured approach to long-term and permanent change that is brought about by revelation of the new demands of God. It is mature interaction with heaven's will in the earth.

This is John's technology. The Lord is coming; His way must be *prepared!* Necessary and definite deliberate action has to be taken if the new thing has to arrive accurately. John announces that a "mightier" appearance is at the doors that will bring a greater manifestation of light and power, but the pathway to that level is through deliberate preparation by a complete renovation and reconfiguration of spiritual mentalities.

We must resist the counterfeit pathways to softer and inaccurate dimensions of revival in the earth. An emotional, self-indulgent experience is not the pathway to stronger and more dominating Church positions. This Reformation that is present today is the declaration and preparation for a greater season of God that is already here in the earth, waiting to be activated by our acceptance of the present apostolic utterance and the vital changing of our hearts. The future move of God in the Church will be the greatest manifestation of His power and presence ever to hit the earth. It will be characterized by winnowing and thorough cleansing of the Body of Christ, the final gathering of all souls named for Christ out of all the nations of the earth and the thrust to the final judgment of all rebellious satanic positions both in the heavens and in the earth. The cry of the Reformation is to NOW prepare!

**"His winnowing fan is in His hand, and He will thoroughly clean out His threshing floor, and gather His wheat into the barn; but He will burn up the chaff with unquenchable fire."**

**Matthew 3:12**

## • *Reformation is not subject to current trends.*

**As they departed, Jesus began to say to the multitudes concerning John: "What did you go out into the wilderness to see? A reed shaken by the wind?**

**But what did you go out to see? A man clothed in soft garments? Indeed, those who wear soft clothing are in kings' houses."**

**Matthew 11:7,8**

Reformation is not a "reed shaken by the wind" of popular opinion or of popular spiritual trends. The core of every genuine Reformation move of God is an apostolic/prophetic impartation of the mind, resources and the grace of God for future positions of the Spirit in the earth. Thus, by definition, a Reformation is bringing into the earth that which is not yet accessed by the ordinary corporate mentality of the Church. It is transformational in nature and introduces the future into the now!

Haggai was raised up by God to break into prevailing mentalities of his day that had caused the building work of the house of God to cease. The popular opinion of the times was that it was the time to build their personal houses but was not the time to build the house of God. The powerful declarations of Haggai released a new season of the Lord's nearness, reversed the trends and activated the process to begin again:

"Thus speaks the LORD of hosts, saying: 'This people says, "The time has not come, the time that the LORD'S house should be built." ' "

Then the word of the LORD came by Haggai the prophet, saying,

"Is it time for you yourselves to dwell in your paneled houses, and this temple to lie in ruins?"

Now therefore, thus says the LORD of hosts: *"Consider your ways!"*

Haggai 1:2-5

Then Zerubbabel the son of Shealtiel, and Joshua the son of Jehozadak, the high priest, with all the remnant of the people, obeyed the voice of the LORD their God, and the words of Haggai the prophet, as the LORD their God had sent him; and the people feared the presence of the LORD.

Then Haggai, the LORD'S messenger, spoke the LORD'S message to the people, saying, "I am with you, says the LORD."

So the LORD stirred up the spirit of Zerubbabel the son of Shealtiel, governor of Judah, and the spirit of Joshua the son of Jehozadak, the high priest, and the

**spirit of all the remnant of the people; and they came and worked on the house of the LORD of hosts, their God,**
**Haggai 1:12-14**

A true Reformation is not clothed in soft garments; it does not operate in comfortable, user-friendly anointings. The word soft is *"malakos"* used to represent a boy selling his body for lewd, homosexual practices. It is that which supposes itself to be male but is in fact perverted maleness. It indicates the prostitution of spiritual positions for religious elevation *(kings' houses)* or popularity. True Reformation is not apparently governmental on the outside but perverted by democratic approval or popular posturings on the inside. This is not what John is and is not to be once found as part of the structure of genuine Reformation.

• *Reformation brings a higher level or rank and becomes the bottom indicator of a new standard.*

**"But what did you go out to see? A prophet? Yes, I say to you, *and more than a prophet.*"**

**"For this is he of whom it is written: 'Behold, I send My messenger before Your face, who will prepare Your way before You.'**

**"Assuredly, I say to you, among those born of women there has not risen one greater than John the Baptist; but he who is least in the kingdom of heaven is greater than he."**
**Matthew 11:9-11**

John is "more than" a prophet. It is interesting to note that John performed no great miracles like Elijah or Elisha. He wrote no books of scripture like Jeremiah or Isaiah. He is not recorded to have experienced any mighty visions of the things of God like Ezekiel, yet he is more than a prophet. "More than" is *"perissoteron*

*(Greek)"*: super-added, exceedingly abundantly, much more remarkable than, exceeding the rank of, superior to. John exceeds in rank the prophets who went before his time.

In this context, the prophets represent the normal moves of God before this time. In Israel the appearance of the prophets was part of the normally accepted spiritual technology by which God spoke to the people. When a prophet appeared in the city, every person, even the children, were aware that God was about to speak. John exceeded the prophets. That which John brought to Israel was not common and within the regular patterns of God's consistent speaking. A Reformation breaks the established patterns of the moves of God in the earth. It is of a higher frequency and has a more devastating spiritual impact. This Reformation is of a higher rank than the successive moves of God that we have experienced up to this time.

There have been wonderful moves of the Spirit in the modern Church. The Pentecostal and Charismatic moves of God have released great blessings into the Body of Christ. The Faith Movement and other movements of the Spirit have released maturity and have enhanced doctrinal positions and operational strength, but this Reformation that is building in the earth is the deepest and most fundamental activity of the Spirit since the Day of Pentecost.

An understanding of the *"perissoteron"* principle helps to properly receive what God is doing in the day of Reformation. We understand that the former standards and expectations that have served us in moves of the former time must be put aside and a more radical position must be taken. If we apply the same standards to the present Reformation, if we seek the operations of

Elisha in John the Baptist we will miss the appearance of God in our time.

There are those who are attempting to access the power of the Reformation today with the mentality principles of former moves of God.  We cannot apply the "bless me" mentalities of the past, and the "my needs" attitudes of the former times to this Reformation.  God is moving by His Spirit in the earth, but His presence is not to be found in the endless quest for manifestation, the entertainment of miracles and ministry spectacles, and the self-validating "feelings" of the Spirit in the midst of church services.  A more severe standard must be applied in the day of Reformation.

In the mountain of re-activation of ministry Elijah sees and hears the mighty manifestations of the wind, the earthquake and the fire as the Lord passed by, but it is in the place of the confrontation of utterance *(the still small voice)* that the clarity of self-analysis and the excitement of new comissioning comes to the tired prophet *(1 Kings 19:11-15)*.

John becomes in his day, the bottom indicator for a future standard for the Kingdom in the earth.  Even the least in the Kingdom will be greater than John and John in his appearance has just revised the former level of the prophets who went before him.  So too Reformation marks the elevation of the general standard of the Church.  The minimum standard of the 21$^{st}$ century Church and the operational levels of the believers of the next millenium are being pushed upward to new positions in this day of Reformation.  We are experiencing a definite departure from the levels of the old order and we will never return.

### • *Reformation creates a new level of spiritual intensity in the Kingdom.*

From the days of John the Baptist until now, the kingdom of heaven has been forcefully advancing, and forceful men lay hold of it.

For all the Prophets and the Law prophesied until John.

And if you are willing to accept it, he is the Elijah who was to come.

He who has ears, let him hear.

**Matthew 11:12-15 (NIV)**

John changed the momentum of Kingdom advance in the earth. His activity brought forth "forceful men" who produced a "forcefully advancing" Kingdom. When the momentum of the Kingdom changes in the season of Reformation, the spiritual characteristics of men must change to come into line with the characteristics of the Kingdom advance. The Kingdom is "forceful" but the men also are "forceful". An "apostolic/prophetic" season cannot be led by men of any other characteristic; a Reformation season requires a Reformation people. The great principle is that for the things of God to advance, every season of divine progress demands the emergence of people of the prescribed mentality.

This mentality update comes through revelation of God's new and prophetic doings in the earth. God never does any new thing unless He first updates the mentality of His people by prophetic impartation so that they can cooperate and walk in line with His initiatives:

Surely the Lord GOD does nothing, unless He reveals His secret to His servants the prophets.

**Amos 3:7**

The true significance and power of this Reformation can only be accessed through discernment. John, in his day, represented the future fullness of the Elijah anointing which would come to the earth in the time of the Lord's imminent return, but you had to be "willing to accept it".

Willing is the word *"thelo"*: *to be resolved or determined to, to take delight or pleasure in a thing.* It combines not only a heart position of determination but also an engagement of the emotions in a sheer delight to be involved in the accurate purposes of God for the time. The word "accept" is *"dechomai"*: *to embrace, to make one's own, to take upon oneself.* These two words clearly define the personal positions in the day of Reformation. An internal attitude is of vital importance if the impartations being released from the heavens find their way into our hearts to bring clarity and discernment of God's new doings. *He who has ears to hear let him hear!*

## • *Kingdom refinement is a Reformation characteristic.*

**"And even now the ax is laid to the root of the trees. Therefore every tree which does not bear good fruit is cut down and thrown into the fire."**

**Matthew 3:10**

John's message was a message of separation and refinement in the Kingdom in order to produce greater effectiveness of the work of the Lord among His people. Productivity is a demand of the John order; fruit must be produced for Kingdom advance. Jesus clearly taught that there are lawless and rebellious elements within the Kingdom that are offensive to God. These will be removed in order to produce and release the true glory of God through His people:

"The Son of Man will send out His angels, and they will gather out of His kingdom all things that offend, and those who practice lawlessness,

and will cast them into the furnace of fire. There will be wailing and gnashing of teeth.

*Then the righteous will shine forth* as the sun in the kingdom of their Father. He who has ears to hear, let him hear!"

Matthew 13:41-43

The shining forth of the righteous is key to the end-time purpose of God. In Isaiah Chapter 60 the activating principle is that there will be a Church in the earth that will be capable of carrying the glory of God to the nations in a way that the nations will see it and be able to respond. "The glory of God will be seen upon you" *(Isaiah 60:2)*. It is because of this visibility through purity and refinement that the nations and their kings begin to approach God bringing gifts and resources that will "ascend with acceptance on my altar" *(verse 7)*.

## The Reformation Environment

"But to what shall I liken this generation? It is like children sitting in the marketplaces and calling to their companions,

and saying: 'We played the flute for you, and you did not dance; we mourned to you, and you did not lament.'

For John came neither eating nor drinking, and they say, 'He has a demon.'

The Son of Man came eating and drinking, and they say, 'Look, a gluttonous man and a wine-bibber, a friend of tax collectors and sinners!' But wisdom is justified by her children."

Matthew 11:16-19

The environment in which Reformation comes forth is one filled with hostility, manipulation and control. The group called "the companions" represents the people of Reformation in and among the Church. This is the group that pilots the new dimensions of God into the earth or the marketplace, the place of the commerce of the spiritual and the merchandise of the anointing. The "children" are creatures of immature perceptions, shallow demands, petulant spirits and wicked hearts. They are religious people controlled by Pharisee spirits that strongly oppose the advance of the boundaries of Kingdom experience.

There are several issues here. There is a demand that the Reformation people be bound to the conformity of the times and be limited to a range of predetermined and predictable responses. The children in fact say: "I play; you dance." There is a generation *(characterized by the children)* that would control the entire pattern of spiritual responses in the earth. It is a "gatekeeper" generation that demands to be the only initiator of all spiritual activity and will not tolerate any deviance from their set patterns. But the prophetic spirit of the Reformation breaks the set activity of the times. It can stand against the conformity and is able to be the architect of a new set of rules for spiritual advance. It is not intimidated by the marketplace activity of the immature. It is both creative and pioneering; it cuts against the culture of its own time; it recognizes neither the flute nor the lament.

It declares, by its alternative prophetic activity and its apostolic strength, that it is not dancing in the day that a dance is declared in the marketplace and it will not mourn in the day of general lament.

The true spirit of such a generation is shown in the parable of Jesus to be an opposing element within the society of the Church. John is declared to be a demon; the Son of Man is declared to be a glutton, wine-bibber a friend of tax collectors and sinners. This mentality attempts to distort the purposes of God in the earth by wrongly defining every possible move of God. It is the same spirit that has condemned as cultist every genuine reforming move of God in the earth since the beginning.

It is impossible to ever please or satisfy the demands of such a generation. John neither eats nor drinks and is condemned. The Son of Man comes eating and drinking and is likewise also condemned. In the end it is only the product of Reformation activity that justifies it as coming directly from the hand of God. Wisdom will be justified by her children.

## The Dividing Line is John

**And when all the people heard Him, even the tax collectors justified God, having been baptized with the baptism of John.**

**But the Pharisees and lawyers rejected the will of God for themselves, not having been baptized by him.**

**Luke 7:29,30**

To be baptised with the baptism of John is to be immersed in the spirit of the Reformation and determines your ability to hear and to receive what is yet to come. When Jesus came with the full power and splendor of God, speaking words that challenged the hearts of men like never before, there were those who were incapable of receiving Him and in rejecting Him, they rejected the future purposes of God for their own lives. Having not accepted the deep inner transformation that John brought to the earth, they lacked the capacity to receive the greater which was now here.

Those who were baptised in John and had been stretched in the inner man, challenged and broken in their traditional legalistic mentalities and expanded in their prophetic perceptions, could receive with joy that for which they had been prepared. They justified God and fully comprehended the activity and purposes of God for their time.

The similar patterns exist in this Reformation move of God today in our generation. We must be baptised in John; we must receive the deep repentance, the mentality renovations and the apostolic/prophetic impartations of this move of God. We must be prepared with global mentalities and unlimited faith to move swiftly with God in the coming glorious days of the 21$^{st}$ century. We must be prepared to enter in and be totally changed now.

## Chapter 4
# The Technology of Reformation

## Technology: A Definition

The term "technology" refers to system of internal spiritual principles and laws that make an external spiritual manifestation predictable and stable. We can apply the principle in the natural also. If you point your remote at the television and press the button the television activates every time without fail. Never do you point a television remote at the television and get a microwave oven: the activity is predictable and stable because of the internal technology of the system. The internal wiring and circuitry of the television set is unique and peculiar to the system and so performs in a reliable way.

A Reformation has certain peculiar characteristics that the modern Church has to come to terms with and begin to understand. It is not a "manifestation" move of God in which something unexpected happens, and people are blessed by immediate movements of the Spirit. A Reformation has to be received as revelation from heaven and progressively built upon the earth by willing and faith-filled saints. For a Reformation to come to maturity and full release of all the intentions and designs of God, people must understand clearly the inner workings, the prescribed mentality and the desired activities

47

and attitudes that cause a move of God to go irresistibly forward. They must understand the technology of a Reformation move in order to create a stable and predictable advance of the Spirit in the earth.

We are now in a different season of the Church. No longer will moves of God sputter out into ineffectiveness, and be entrapped and fossilized in organized religion, constitutions, religious codes and laws. The apostolic, sent mentality that is now gripping the Church is demanding that a people be birthed that have the mentality and capability to finish the purposes of God:

> **Jesus said to them, "My food is to do the will of Him who sent Me and to finish His work.**
>
> **John 4:34**

The times and seasons of the earth have to be brought to a state of fullness of completion so that Jesus can accomplish all His desires. It is our responsibility as co-workers with God *(1 Corinthians 3:9)* to ensure that the fullest potential of every move of God is swiftly reached in the earth.

> **...that in the dispensation of the fullness of the times He might gather together in one all things in Christ, both which are in heaven and which are on earth — in Him.**
>
> **Ephesians 1:10**

# Reformation and Prophetic Insight

We have already seen that the word "reformation" implies a right arrangement or ordering of things, a restoration or an amendment and indicates a time when the imperfect or the inadequate would be superseded by a better order of things.

In *Acts 24:2* there is a further amplification of some of the conditions that surround effective reformation:

When Paul was called in, Tertullus presented his case before Felix: "We have enjoyed a long period of peace under you, and your foresight has brought about reforms in this nation.

**Acts 24:2 (NIV)**

Here Paul has been brought before Felix, the governor of Judea, and evidence against him is being given by Tertullus the orator. Though the application here is in a secular situation, it nevertheless serves to add to our understanding of reformation conditions. Tertullus speaks of reforms *(prosperity: NKJ)* that have been brought to the nation through "foresight". The word foresight refers to the ability to see ahead and understand the conditions of the future and thus having the ability to act accurately and effectively in the present. We can adjust our powerful activity in the present because our present action is linked to a future reality. Thus, Reformation is activated by a prophetic people, who live from the future back into the present.

This is part of the core mentality of today's Reformation Church. We have moved into the finishing mentality of the apostolic spirit *(John 4:34)*. We are now viewing in our spirit the end or finish of all things, and so we construct a powerful present full of the unfolding purposes of God, that provides a platform to effectively invade the future.

# Active Technology:
# Isolating Reformation Principles

Because *finding fault with them,* He says: "Behold, the days are coming, says the Lord, when I will make a new covenant with the house of Israel and with the house of Judah —

*"not according to the covenant* that I made with their fathers in the day when I took them by the hand

to lead them out of the land of Egypt; because they did not continue in My covenant, and I disregarded them, says the Lord.

"For this is the covenant that I will make with the house of Israel after those days, says the Lord: I will *put My laws in their mind and write them on their hearts;* and *I will be their God, and they shall be My people.*

"None of them shall teach his neighbor, and none his brother, saying, 'Know the Lord,' *for all shall know Me, from the least of them to the greatest* of them.

"For I will be merciful to their unrighteousness, and their sins and *their lawless deeds I will remember no more."*

In that He says, "A new covenant," He has made the first obsolete. Now *what is becoming obsolete* and growing old is ready to vanish away.

**Hebrews 8:8-13**

Again we are seeking Reformation technology in what may have been the greatest shift in the entire history of the human race on this planet — the move from law to grace. Here God is rewriting the rulebook, providing an entirely new constitution which will guide His relationship with men. Things are being invalidated, but new things are being constructed in the heavens and in the hearts of men. We will look into the operations of this shift and find active principles that are still valid in God's operations today. The term "active technology" points to certain operational principles that were used in the past in pattern reformations, which had an effectiveness that was greater than the situations in which they appeared. These principles which we will now identify and discuss are still in operation today. They have been lying unattended for generations but will now spring to life as they are understood and activated in our 21$^{st}$ Reformation.

### • Reformation Principle One: Reformation is "not according" to what went before (verse 9).

The basis for constructing a move or operation of God that is not according to what went before is that God found fault with the present system. *The word translated "finding fault" implies that the present system that is being invalidated is still in operation, but must now be tested with a higher order of insight.* We are not finding fault because of a critical spirit, but because a new and higher level of perception, desire and understanding is being applied to the present system. This is very important to note because it points to the heart of a reformation move of God.

Martin Luther was not a destructive outsider who came to attack the Catholic monolith. He was a faithful monk, who from the inside attained a higher level of insight and began to biblically "find fault" with the system. Unless the "faultfinding" proceeds out of this level it will not bring life. Reformation people within a system are filled with a demand that has come directly from God. It is God who invalidates what He has formerly built. The Old Covenant was from God but so was the New. The shift is from that which was God, to that which is now God; the entire technology of Reformation takes place within the parameters of God's activity and dealings. No fleshly criticism or carnal desires must be allowed to enter. Our "finding fault" must be of the Spirit only and not of the flesh.

Therefore the new thing that is built is "not according" to that which went before. "Not according" can also be translated "not deriving from". It is important

51

that we understand how this applies in our context. We must not destroy the biblical and doctrinal gains of the past generations and dismantle the past positions of the faith. God has always been in the process of restoring the Church. However, a Reformation involves the creation of a platform of entirely new mentalities and worldviews which do not derive from the mentalities of past operations of the Church.

> Then He spoke a parable to them: "No one puts a piece from a new garment on an old one; *otherwise the new makes a tear,* and also the piece that was taken out of *the new does not match the old.*
>
> And no one puts new wine into old wineskins; or else the new wine will burst the wineskins and be spilled, and the wineskins will be ruined.
>
> But new wine must be put into new wineskins, and both are preserved.
>
> And no one, having drunk old wine, immediately desires new; for he says, 'The old is better.'"
>
> Luke 5:36-39

> "Do not remember the former things, nor consider the things of old.
>
> Behold, *I will do a new thing,* now it shall spring forth; shall you not know it?....
>
> ....*to give drink to My people,* My chosen."
>
> Isaiah 43:18-20

The spiritual perspectives being built now in the earth will seem strange, new and radical to the traditionalists of the Church because in fact they are. David's Tabernacle must have seemed strange to those of the Mosaic order. In fact Michal, Saul's daughter who was David's wife, could not tolerate his apparently "unkingly" behavior *(2 Samuel 6:16).* She was entirely unaware that the standard for kingliness had changed with the introduction of the order of the Tabernacle.

**• *Reformation Principle Two: The law is written in the mind and the heart (verse 10).***

The direction of a Reformation is always inward to a stronger position of God within the heart of men. Though the days of Reformation may cause mighty manifestations of the power of God, manifestation without inner restructuring is worthless. Reformation is a greater demonstration of the proximity of the Kingdom. John the Baptist came with a simple and direct message — the Kingdom of God was near. What was required he called "repentance" — the dealings of God in the heart. A true Kingdom impact is not primarily external but internal:

> Now when He was asked by the Pharisees when the kingdom of God would come, He answered them and said, "The kingdom of God does not come with observation;
>
> nor will they say, 'See here!' or 'See there!' For indeed, the kingdom of God is within you."
>
> Luke 17:20,21

This aspect of the internal focus of a Reformation movement is seen in the Reformation conducted by King Hezekiah *(2 Chronicles 29:29)*. He acts against a backdrop of moral decline in Judah *(2 Chronicles 28:19)*, and identifies his priority as internal cleansing, carrying out the rubbish from the holy place. The direction of his cleansing is from the inside to the outside:

> Then the priests went into the inner part of the house of the LORD to cleanse it, and brought out all the debris that they found in the temple of the LORD

to the court of the house of the LORD. And the Levites took it out and carried it to the Brook Kidron.

Now they began to sanctify on the first day of the first month, and on the eighth day of the month they came to the vestibule of the LORD.

2 Chronicles 29:16,17

There are two important dimensions to Hezekiah's move:

"Moreover all the articles which King Ahaz in his reign had cast aside in his transgression we have *prepared* and *sanctified;* and there they are, before the altar of the LORD."

2 Chronicles 29:19

"Sanctified" means to set apart, to make sacred or to hallow, and this represents the powerful internal work that takes place in the heart. There must be a greater dimension of holiness within. "Prepared" means to stabilize into a good arrangement, to fix properly, to cause to stand up perpendicular, to establish. This speaks of the correction of the laxness and weakness of the mind to cause it to be properly established in biblical patterns so that absolute obedience could result.

The law or the current constitution of God for the present move must be inscribed or written on the heart and mind. Acceptance of and obedience to the current positions must not be the result of regulation, but must flow from strong desire for the order of God from within. To put it simply, God wants to reconnect powerfully with the hearts of His people once again in this Reformation.

• *Reformation Principle Three: Re-establishment of Divine Intimacy (verse 10).*

The result of the reconnection of the "law" with the heart of man will be the re-establishment of intimacy between man and God. This was the first great reality that was destroyed by disobedience in the times of Adam. He could no longer bear relationship with God and hid himself from the face of God. Fear replaced trust and a focus on self destroyed his focus on God. He became absorbed with covering his own nakedness and hid in the bushes from God. The question from God that still hangs in the environment of the generations is — "Who told you that you were naked?" (Genesis 3:11).

Adam did not become naked as a result of disobedience. He was always naked but never realized it because his God-focus was more powerful than his self-focus. Intimacy destroyed earthly frequencies and introduced him, even while he lived on this earth, into a more refined environment of awareness in which God filled His gaze.

Reformation draws us God-ward once again. In the process of this our carnal perceptions are destroyed and we are introduced into the environment of the purposes of God. Church built on carnal, earthly ambitions is dismantled in favor of Church built upon the progress of the purposes of God. We go beyond religion to intimacy; He will be our God and we will be His people.

Reformation intimacy is a powerful thing. It brings us beyond the limitations and hindrances that keep us separate from Him (the windows and the lattice) into a world beyond discouragement and barrenness into a time of fruitfulness, birthing and the singing of the turtledove (Holy Spirit).

**The voice of my beloved! Behold, he comes leaping upon the mountains, skipping upon the hills.**

**My beloved is like a gazelle or a young stag. Behold, he stands behind our wall; he is looking through the windows, gazing through the lattice.**

My beloved spoke, and said to me: *"Rise up, my love, my fair one, and come away.*

For lo, the winter is past, the rain is over and gone.

The flowers appear on the earth; the time of singing has come, and the voice of the turtledove is heard in our land.

The tender grapes give a good smell. Rise up, my love, my fair one, and come away!*

**Song of Solomon 2:8-13**

## • *Reformation Principle Four: Issues of revelation equalization (verse 11).*

Part of the process of a Reformation is to break the imbalances of revelation and understanding and to bring an equal opportunity to all people. There must be no nation, culture or people that have an advantage in accessing the mysteries of the Kingdom. The access stipulated by Jesus never raised up one group within the Church above another. Access was given to the entire Church as opposed to those outside the Kingdom:

He answered and said to them, "Because it has been given to you to know the mysteries of the kingdom of heaven, but to them it has not been given."

**Matthew 13:11**

During the days of the Protestant Reformation, Luther demanded that the Bible be printed so that all men might have access to the written word of God. This demand created horror in the hearts of those religious people, who used restricted access and ignorance of the masses to exercise lordship and spiritual dominion over them. In our day we have seen the development of what can only be called "imperialist Christianity" and "patronizing relationships" by assumed enlightened sectors of the Church over the assumed ignorant sectors of the Church. As in Luther's day, so too in ours, Reformation comes to break the imbalances: *"all shall know Me from the least of them to the greatest of them"*.

There is undoubtedly today an endtime prophetic emphasis of the Spirit in the so-called "Third World". There are those in the Third World nations who have, in a distorted backlash of a racist gospel, erred in designating the Spirit's emphasis declaring that Jesus now will use only black people. This is not the gospel of the Kingdom. It is not only shortsighted, but also discriminatory, given the variety of peoples upon this planet. But it is clearly evident that there is a mighty surge of endtime Reformation emphasis in the nations of the Third World, which is connecting with surges of the moves of God coming out of other areas of the earth:

**"And in that day there shall be a Root of Jesse, who shall stand as a banner to the people; for the Gentiles shall seek Him, and His resting place shall be glorious."**

**It shall come to pass in that day that the LORD shall set His hand again the second time to recover the remnant of His people who are left, from Assyria and Egypt, from Pathros and Cush, from Elam and Shinar, from Hamath and the islands of the sea.**

**He will set up a banner for the nations, and will assemble the outcasts of Israel, and gather together the dispersed of Judah from the four corners of the earth.**
**Isaiah 11:10-12**

The nations indicated here as God sets up a banner for the nations undoubtedly point to a focus of the Spirit on "Third World" areas of the earth. We must understand that we must work for the maturing of the Church in all areas of the earth, so that a fully formed and complete expression and revelation of Christ emerges out of every society. This too is part of the Reformation.

• *Reformation Principle Five: The power of a prophetic declaration (verse 13).*

*In that He says, "A new covenant," He has made the first obsolete.*

It is the announcement of the new that initiates the destruction of the old. It is the *"saying"* that is the *"making"*. Essential to the forming of a Reformation in the earth must be the prophetic declaration of what is to come forth. Great spiritual dynamics are released as the prophetic people begin the urgent declaration in the earth of the current moves of God and present positions of the Spirit.

When God was about to bring His people out of Babylon, ending seventy years of bondage and servitude, introducing them to a new day of building in the purposes of God, He issued instructions through the mouth of prophet Jeremiah releasing the technology for the passage into the new day:

> **"Declare among the nations, proclaim, and set up a standard; proclaim — *do not conceal it* — say, "Babylon is taken, Bel is shamed. Merodach is broken in pieces; her idols are humiliated, her images are broken in pieces."**
>
> **For out of the north a nation comes up against her, which shall make her land desolate, and no one shall dwell therein. They shall move, they shall depart, both man and beast."**
>
> **"In those days and in that time," says the LORD, "The children of Israel shall come, they and the children of Judah together; with continual weeping they shall come, and seek the LORD their God."**
>
> **Jeremiah 50:2-4**

They must begin to speak prophetically and declare that Bel and Merodach are already shamed and broken.

They were commanded not to conceal that which God would do. It is interesting to note that at the time they were commanded to speak that there were no actual signs that the Babylonian system was coming under the judgment of the Lord. Their prophetic utterance would create the spiritual dynamics that would eventually manifest as political crisis in Babylon.

The powerful principle for Reformation here is that the declaration inside the system of the emergence of the new thing, shakes the foundations of that which is old and releases the purposes of God. All across the earth today, in many nations and societies, the prophetic people are filling out their Reformation desires with apostolic doctrine and expressing their Reformation order in apostolic networks. Both their utterance and their activity are prophetic. The new order of the 21$^{st}$ century Church is being expressed in the earth in a powerful Reformation because we have "said".

### • *Reformation Principle Six: Conditions of obsolescence (verse 13).*

In the great shift to the New Covenant the first covenant was made obsolete. The word "obsolete" in its original language means "worn out by time and use". It refers to a heavenly release that is no longer relevant to the present seasons in the earth. All the religious complexity of the ritual sacrificial system was revealed to be a "copy and a shadow". All of this was produced in the earth by divine instruction to Moses by God, but in the days of that Reformation, things which were once divine instruction were made useless and irrelevant to the times.

Often people refuse to move into the new things being released by the Spirit because they are locked into old paradigms, and pictures of the days of past breakthroughs still live in their memory. They feel that if they release that which was once life giving and migrate to new positions that they are being unfaithful to what God once did in their lives. Their desire for the old remains unchecked:

**"But new wine must be put into new wineskins, and both are preserved."**

**"And no one, having drunk old wine, immediately desires new; *for he says, 'The old is better.'"***
**Luke 5:38,39**

The key to Reformation migration is that we must realize that God Himself will declare many of the past positions to be obsolete as He releases newer, more accurate and more effective positions in the earth. We must be open to more productive and purpose-driven types of covenant relationships; new organizational structures being developed in the Church; new vocabulary, tuning into the frequencies of a 21$^{st}$ century generation; new behavioral leadership patterns and fresh management initiatives in the modern Church as we move to brand new places of power in the earth.

The things that are declared by heaven to be obsolete because of a prophetic declaration of the new thing will "vanish away". It is pointless to continue to build upon that which is dated and condemned to be consumed. All structures, mentalities and spiritual positions which no longer carry the freshness of God for the times, will progressively "grow old" and will in the end fragment and "vanish away".

## Further Reformation Principles

Let us now zoom into an even more intricate dimension of the technology of Reformation, and extract living principles out of the design and operation of the Tabernacle of Moses itself:

Now when these things had been thus prepared, the priests always went into the first part of the tabernacle, performing the services.

But into the second part the high priest went alone once a year, not without blood, which he offered for himself and for the people's sins committed in ignorance;

*the Holy Spirit indicating this,* that the way into the Holiest of All was *not yet made manifest* while the first tabernacle was still standing.

*It was symbolic for the present time* in which both gifts and sacrifices are offered *which cannot make him who performed the service perfect* in regard to the conscience —

concerned only with foods and drinks, various washings, and fleshly ordinances imposed until the time of reformation.

But Christ came as High Priest of *the good things to come....*

**Hebrews 9:6-11**

• *Reformation Principle Seven: The limitation of the system (verse 9).*

*"...cannot make him who performed the service perfect in regard to the conscience —"*

The problem that existed was that even if the activity of Moses' Tabernacle was fine-tuned to maximum effectiveness and efficiency; if each and every regulation was followed with all possible exactness, it could only cleanse the flesh and could never penetrate to effective cleansing of the conscience. However the demand of the worshipper was to have his conscience cleansed. When a system, even if pushed to the extremes of effectiveness, still *"cannot make"* those who participate in it fulfilled in their spiritual demands, then the only alternative is a move to Reformation and the implementation of a more effective system.

Again the direction of a Reformation's effectiveness is always to a more inward position. The movements of the Spirit among the people of God are always to capture a greater place in the hearts of men. The moves of God always plunge inward to the core of man's being: the glory wants to rest in the inner temple. The "cleansing of the flesh" represents a limitation to a more exteriorized position; the "cleansing of the conscience" represents a new power to thrust inward to the heart of man. The people of a season of Reformation are a people who elevate the demand of the heart above the cry of the flesh. They give greater value to the inner work of the Spirit over the outward manifestation.

Spiritual frustration and unfulfilled spiritual desire constitute the pulsating core of a Reformation. Demand must exceed the present system's ability: hunger must grow more intense than the spiritual supply. The outflow of heaven's resources into the earth must exceed the capacity of the Church's present system to receive. This is an active Reformation dynamic.

## • *Reformation Principle Eight: Dynamics of replacement (verse 8).*

"...the way...was not yet made manifest while the first...was still standing."

The High Priest's entrance into the second part of Moses Tabernacle once a year with blood, represented a principle of limited access. This was built into the system erected by Mosaic decree. This very limitation points to an important piece of Reformation technology. It was the Holy Spirit speaking here; this was an indication directly from heaven. As long as the first tabernacle was operational or "still standing," the way into the true tabernacle, the Holiest of All could not be made manifest.

"Manifest" is: *to be made actual, visible, to be recognized or to be understood.* The word carries implications of not only operation but also revelation. As long as the principles or mentalities of the insufficient present system retained their hold and authority upon the minds of the worshippers, neither the operations nor the revelation understanding of the new would be released. The Holy Spirit indicated that the new could not be released until the old was challenged and began to fragment.

This essential change is part of the process of Reformation and both processes are happening at the same time: one order is failing while another order is rising to replace it. The opinion of the times that you hear is dependent upon which perspective you have access to. Reformation brings within the system a sense of conflict that really is the dynamic order of change:

> **Now there was a long war between the house of Saul and the house of David. But David grew stronger and stronger, and the house of Saul grew weaker and weaker.**                                       **2 Samuel 3:1**

Every governmental form transmits a mentality. Every Reformation brings with it a new mentality and new patterns of operations, music, prayer, lifestyle, personal identity and executive ability of the Spirit in the earth. The old patterns must fragment and pass away and the new mentalities of the new order must begin to emerge in the earth.

• *Reformation Principle Nine: Issues concerning liberty (verse 10).*
*"...ordinances imposed until...."*

In the day of Reformation, the old system becomes an imposition. That which was formerly the bringer of life becomes the harbinger of bondage. The word "imposed" means: to press upon, to lie upon, to place on top of.

When Joseph brought his father Jacob and his brothers into the land of Egypt, it was to inherit a great blessing and to preserve their life:

> So Israel dwelt in the land of Egypt, in the country of Goshen; and they had possessions there and grew and multiplied exceedingly.
>
> **Genesis 47:27**

By the time of Moses, the land of Goshen was no longer a place of life but had become a land of imposition. Servitude had replaced favor; bitterness had replaced hope:

> Therefore they set taskmasters over them to afflict them with their burdens. And they built for Pharaoh supply cities, Pithom and Raamses.
>
> And they made their lives bitter with hard bondage — in mortar, in brick, and in all manner of service in the field. All their service in which they made them serve was with rigor.
>
> **Exodus 1:11,14**

God raised up Moses to bring a great deliverance to the people. The cry of God in the midst of the Reformation led by Moses is the enduring cry of God in the midst of every Reformation the earth has ever seen. It is the demand that the servitude be broken, that the people be released:

> And the LORD spoke to Moses, "Go to Pharaoh and say to him, '"Thus says the LORD: "Let My people go, that they may serve Me."
>
> **Exodus 8:1**

Servitude continues "until" Reformation. Within every genuine Reformation there must be a commitment to freedom. The people must be guided towards a relevant and deeper encounter with God: they must come to serve Him.

Elijah the prophet brought a great Reformation to Israel, destroying the impositions of Baal-worship in the lives of the people. The heart-cry of Elijah, in the midst of the awesome happenings on Mount Carmel, was that things performed in the earth at the bidding of God, would cause an open realization in the saints that God was truly and demonstrably a great God. Elijah desired that their hearts would once again turn to Him.

**And it came to pass, at the time of the offering of the evening sacrifice, that Elijah the prophet came near and said, "LORD God of Abraham, Isaac, and Israel, let it be known this day that You are God in Israel and I am Your servant, and that I have done all these things at Your word.**

**"Hear me, O LORD, hear me, that this people may know that You are the LORD God, and that You have turned their hearts back to You again."**
**1 Kings 18:36,37**

Reformation lifts the banner of a new level of spiritual release and freedom over a people committed to a closer approach to God.

• *Reformation Principle Ten: There is a time of Reformation (verse 10).*

Reformation has a set season in the mind of God. The word "time" is the word *"kairos"*. Kairos is a fixed and definite time when things are brought to crisis. It is a long-awaited decisive epoch; a time constituted with certain set events. The implication of the word "constituted," is that the period of the kairos has built into it a certain sequence of events which have to be brought forth and completed in the earth in order for the kairos to be complete. It is impossible to separate a kairos from the events that characterize it. The time literally demands that certain actions follow.

Kairos emphasizes not the convenience of the season, but the absolute necessity of the task at hand whether the time provides a convenient opportunity or not. Thus the mentality that produces activity in the day of Reformation is a mentality that is seamlessly joined to the producing of the desire of God in the earth, denying the demand of the flesh for comfort, convenience or ease.

Because of this, Reformation exists in a spiritual environment that is highly charged with a sense of urgency that breaks out of the complacency of the time. Reformers perceive the crisis that others do not detect and issue the prophetic cry for people to come forward to the next level in God. Reformation is robust spiritual activity that will not tolerate hindrance or religious resistance. It is filled with sacrificial activity and impregnated with a sense of destiny. In the day of Reformation, ordinary saints are elevated to the awareness of the purposes of God and come to clarity of their own significance in the global plan.

The power of God and the revelation of God are both bound up in the kairos. Moses in the heat of expectation and desire acted outside the parameters of the kairos of deliverance and killed an Egyptian. His desire was accurate but his timing was wrong. He was not yet positioned inside the kairos of God: the power needed to shake an empire just did not flow. Defeated and afraid he fled into the wilderness for forty years.

When God's time arrived he was intercepted by God, equipped and prepared with a message, and empowered with the resources from heaven to destroy the stubborn pride of Pharaoh. Inside the kairos of Reformation the mighty power of God is released and displayed to bring His plans to pass.

# Reformation Keys

### • *Key One: We must enter into newness.*

And Moses said: "By this you shall know that the LORD has sent me to do all these works, for I have not done them of my own will.

If these men die naturally like all men, or if they are visited by the common fate of all men, then the LORD has not sent me."

*"But if the LORD creates a new thing, and the earth opens its mouth and swallows them up with* all that belongs to them, and they go down alive into the pit, then you will understand that these men have rejected the LORD."

**Numbers 16:28-30**

The wind of newness is a sign that a sending from the Lord has taken place. Newness involves the breakage of that which is traditional and which is expected and usual. It is the producing of outcomes not expected by the community. God always moves in the midst of that which is new. We are encouraged in scripture to sing to the Lord a "new" song (Psalm 144:9;96:1;98:1). God is elevated in the midst of expression that is fresh and emerging in the now! The "new" song points to a dimension of creativity and a current response to God that is not connected to the stifling patterns of traditional response.

God's continuous pattern is to go beyond that which has already been manifested and to anchor His people in a brand-new experience:

"Behold, the former things have come to pass, and *new things I declare;* before they spring forth I tell you of them."

> *Sing to the LORD a new song,* **and His praise from the ends of the earth, you who go down to the sea, and all that is in it, you coastlands and you inhabitants of them!**
>
> Isaiah 42:9,10

When God begins to declare a new thing because the former is now no longer current, the people of God must in that season begin to "sing" a song that is "new". They must lift up an utterance that is of the same frequency with the current new speaking of God.

### • *Key Two: Manifest an end-time mentality.*

The apostolic mentality of an end-time Reformation people breaks the expected product cycle of the earth. Satan is also working towards a harvest of mentalities. He ploughs up the minds of men with error, pride, laziness and complacency, and every evil unbelieving work. He expects to harvest predictable attitudes, positions and mentalities that make it impossible for the Kingdom of God to advance. A Reformation is a major blossoming of accurate divine mentalities (*1 Corinthians 2:16*) in the midst of a satanically controlled earth.

The cry of Isaiah to a Reformation people identifies the creation of oppositional mentalities in a darkening earth:

> **Arise, shine; for your light has come! And the glory of the LORD is risen upon you.**
>
> **For behold, the darkness shall cover the earth, and deep darkness the people; but the LORD will arise over you, and His glory will be seen upon you.**
>
> **The Gentiles shall come to your light, and kings to the brightness of your rising.**
>
> Isaiah 60:1-3

To the people of the earth it is the time of sunset-darkness is about to cover the earth and a blanket of ignorance is shrouding their mentalities. But to the people of the Reformation it is sunrise. They live in a totally opposite experience within the same physical context. In the midst of Satan's darkness the glory of God is being seen and the dawning of His radiance in His people draws the nations toward a fresh revelation of His power. Such is the strength of a Reformation.

### • *Key Three: Receive revelation power for a new lifestyle.*

"On that day I will raise up the tabernacle of David, which has fallen down, and repair its damages; I will raise up its ruins, and rebuild it as in the days of old;

That they may possess the remnant of Edom, and all the Gentiles (nations) who are called by My name," says the LORD who does this thing.

**Amos 9:11,12**

We will deal with the Reformation principles resident in the Tabernacle of David in a later chapter of this book. However the spiritual systems that upheld the type of radical lifestyle represented by the tent erected by David will be rebuilt in the end-time earth. David's tent offers the technology to erect advanced spiritual positions as a fifth column within the prevailing traditional and religious systems of the earth.

It will cause all nations named of the Lord to come into possession of their spiritual inheritance. All spiritual enemies who have escaped the assaults of the Church in past moves of God will be given into the hand of the Reformation people who live under the principles of the rebuilt tabernacle.

# Chapter 5
# Strategies for Reformation Breakthrough

*R*ead Isaiah Chapters 61 and 62.

These chapters deal extensively with the Reformation process and lead us to strategies for a Reformation breakthrough. Isaiah describes the spiritual resources of the Messiah or the "anointed" one. The word "Messiah" is rendered "Christos" or Christ in the New Testament and so the dimensions of the Spirit mentioned here apply to the Christ resource that is producing a certain kind of people in our day called *"trees of righteousness, the planting of the Lord"*.

## Characteristics of Reformation People

In Isaiah 61:9 those that God has raised up in the midst of Reformation are called the *"posterity whom the Lord has blessed"*. Let us examine some characteristics of such people.

• *The blessed posterity are the people of the Reformation who come forth in an acceptable time and in the day of vengeance:*

> To proclaim the acceptable year of the LORD, and the day of vengeance of our God; to comfort all who mourn,
>
> Isaiah 61:2

71

These two dynamics occur together in the day of Reformation. It is both the acceptable time and a season of the Lord's vengeance, and both of these are vital for the construction of adequate Reformation mentality in this season.

The word "acceptable" is the Hebrew word "ratson": *the fullness of divine favor upon His people.* It identifies a season, in which God begins to download all of His covenant promises and graces, upon a people that have entered into an accurate season of powerful receptivity and readiness. It describes a time when spiritual desolation is attacked by a people with a word of global deliverance in their mouths releasing a prophetic statement to the nations of the earth:

> Thus says the LORD: "In *an acceptable time* I have heard You, and in the day of salvation I have helped You; I will preserve You and give You as a covenant to the people, *to restore the earth, to cause them to inherit the desolate heritages;*
>
> That You may say to the prisoners, 'Go forth,' to those who are in darkness, 'Show yourselves.' "They shall feed along the roads, and their pastures shall be on all desolate heights.
> **Isaiah 49:8,9**

Spiritual ability, readiness and positioning are required in the people that receive the "favor" of the Lord. The Lord's "favor" will be released only to a "wise" people:

> The king's *favor* (ratson) is toward *a wise servant,* but his wrath is against him who causes shame.
> **Proverbs 14:35**

It is also the day of vengeance, because the season of the Lord's favor upon His people is also the time when the wrath of the Lord comes against all things that oppose the Kingdom, and resist the ultimate purposes of God in the heart:

72

> For He put on righteousness as a breastplate, and a helmet of salvation on His head; *he put on the garments of vengeance for clothing,* and was clad with zeal as a cloak.
>
> According to their deeds, accordingly He will repay, fury to His adversaries, recompense to His enemies; the coastlands He will fully repay.
>
> Isaiah 59:17,18

The Lord's glory cannot be divorced from vengeance; His majesty in the season of Reformation cannot be separated from judgement.

> Who is this who comes from Edom, with dyed garments from Bozrah, this One who *is glorious in His apparel,* traveling in the greatness of His strength?....
>
> For *the day of vengeance is in My heart,* and the year of My redeemed has come.
>
> Isaiah 63:1-4

• *The blessed posterity is a generation of repairers and rebuilders.*

> And they shall rebuild the old ruins, they shall raise up the former desolations, and they shall repair the ruined cities, the desolations of many generations.
>
> Isaiah 61:4

The combination of words used here implies the activity of rebuilding, making new and establishing. It describes restorative activity that is intent on changing the face of the present system. It assumes that the present state of things has in fact fallen into ruin and disrepair, and that the failure is endemic and deep, the product of many generations. Thus, reformation is not a surface or trivial activity. It pushes to the core reality of the nature of human life that has in fact deteriorated over a long period of time.

The word *"desolations"* has a meaning that implies something that is so awful that it is stunning and appalling. The impact of the blessed posterity is to reverse the deep, appalling failures in the Church and to bring the "cities" back to their former power.

• *The blessed posterity are a people of mighty witness.*

> But you shall be named *the priests* of the LORD, they shall call you *the servants* of our God. You shall eat the riches of the Gentiles, and in their glory you shall boast.
>
> Isaiah 61:6

> "Their descendants shall be known among the Gentiles, and their offspring among the people. All who see them shall acknowledge them, that they are the posterity whom the LORD has blessed."
>
> Isaiah 61:9

These scriptures apply prophetically to our own time of Reformation. There will be a generation of people produced in the Church, which will be of renown in the nations of the earth. These people will be a product of the Reformation mentality and position. They will be the offspring and descendants of what is coming powerfully into the earth now. They will be priests, having mighty spiritual potency and relevance. They will be servants, possessing awesome ability to do the work of the Kingdom and to serve the purposes of the Lord.

• *The blessed posterity is a generation of accurate purpose.*

> "For I, the LORD, love justice; I hate robbery for burnt offering; *I will direct their work in truth,* and will make with them an everlasting covenant."
>
> Isaiah 61:8

The activity of the Reformation generation will proceed in that which is right, faithful, reliable and stable. It describes a people that have removed themselves from works which do not carry the authentic stamp of the Lord's approval. The work of the Church in the day of Reformation will carry the signature of truth. In the Septuagint *(Greek translation of the Bible)* the word *"truth"* speaks of that which lies at the core of all outward manifestation. It describes the verifiable substance of all that is external, the core matter of that which is manifested in the earth.

A Reformation Church returns to the demonstration of a faith that no longer majors on the fluff of an outward manifestation that denies adherence to core values. That, in fact, is an Antichrist principle. Paul speaks of the "lawless one" who displays a dimension of ministry that does not elevate the "truth":

> **The coming of the lawless one is according to the working of Satan, with all power, signs, and lying wonders,**
>
> **and with all unrighteous deception among those who perish, because they did not receive the love of the truth, that they might be saved.**
>
> **2 Thessalonians 2:9,10**

The love of the truth must be received in the hearts of an established people in order to save them from the ravages of deception in the last day. All righteous positions must be established in the "truth" position of the "doctrine of Christ" *(2 John 9)*, and not in the realm of gift-manifestation and proliferation of signs. Such positions open the Church to be deceived by manifestation without a progress into the deep purposes of the Lord. The Reformation people will recover such positions of strength.

# Dynamics of Reformation Productivity

> For as the earth brings forth its bud, as the garden
> causes the things that are sown in it to spring forth, so
> the Lord GOD will cause righteousness and praise to
> spring forth before all the nations.
>
> Isaiah 61:11

Righteousness and praise will spring forth before all
nations. This is prophetically promised to us, but there
is an implied conditionality here. The activation of these
spiritual values in the nations is likened to a garden.
Only that which is first sown in it will eventually spring
forth. If the Lord has to cause a springing forth of certain manifestations of His power and truth in the
nations, there first must be Reformation people who
have the capacity to act in accordance with prophetic
promises.

Several things are implied here. A Reformation
people act in responsibility. They are the custodians of
the prophetic promises. Their activity in the earth has a
direct impact upon the emergence of the prophetic
promises into visible reality. Reformation people are
infused with an apostolic and prophetic spirit because
they have seen in the spirit the eventual purposes of God
and they act in accuracy to design and build it. Only
that which is first sown will eventually spring forth into
open manifestation before the nations.

That which is sown is only the seed of that which is
to come. In the springing forth there is great multiplica-
tion and amplification of the original seed. After the
same fashion, God will cause a great acceleration and
amplification of the seeds of the apostolic and prophetic
activity of the Reformation Church. As Isaiah indicated,
it will be displayed before all the nations.

# Five Breakthrough Strategies

**Go through, go through the gates! Prepare the way for the people; build up, build up the highway! Take out the stones, lift up a banner for the peoples!**

**Isaiah 62:10**

## • *Strategy One: Go through the gates.*

In our traditional understanding gates have always referred to satanic strongholds, but here they refer to the gates of the Lord. God is the inventor of stronghold positions, places of strength and power into which we can be established.

**Open to me the gates of righteousness; I will go through them, and I will praise the LORD.**

**This is the gate of the LORD, through which the righteous shall enter.**

**I will praise You, for You have answered me, and have become my salvation.**

**The stone which the builders rejected has become the chief cornerstone.**

**This was the LORD'S doing; it is marvelous in our eyes.**

**This is the day the LORD has made; we will rejoice and be glad in it.**

**Save now, I pray, O LORD; O LORD, I pray, send now prosperity.**

**Blessed is he who comes in the name of the LORD! We have blessed you from the house of the LORD.**

**Psalm 118:19-26**

This is the last psalm in a series called the "Hallel" and was traditionally sung as the people were in procession up to the gates of the temple. It is more than likely that the procession was timed so that as the crowd approached the gates, they cried out in the psalm for the gates to be opened to them. Thus the gates swinging open to admit the worshippers were synonymous with an entrance into the presence of God Himself. The day which was made by the Lord then became the day of access to His presence. It was a day in which the gates swung open for new admittance.

We can imagine the awesome spectacle. The people advance with songs of praise from the psalms of David. It is a holy procession, which will climax with a shout for the gates to be opened for access to the presence of God. As the huge gates swing slowly open, the people begin to proclaim with all their might: *"Blessed is he who comes in the name of the Lord"*. This is their utterance at the point of entry.

This statement is significant and carries prophetic overtones for the Reformation generation of the present. In *Matthew Chapter 23*, Jesus has been speaking against the Pharisees declaring them to be hypocrites and fools. The Pharisee spirit is established in positions of pride and external works. It is filled with duplicity and spiritual death. It resists the speaking of God in the Church by exterminating the prophetic dimension among God's people *(verse 29-31)*. But its most deadly work is that it shuts up the Kingdom, refuses to enter and bars those who wish to enter unto God. The issue here is one of access; the gates to God are closed.

> **"But woe to you, scribes and Pharisees, hypocrites! For you shut up the kingdom of heaven against men; for you neither go in yourselves, nor do you allow those who are entering to go in."**
>
> **Matthew 23:13**

In the midst of this tirade against the Pharisees, Jesus lifts up His voice in a lament over Jerusalem. In the prophetic application His words carry meaning for the Church.

> "O Jerusalem, Jerusalem, the one who kills the prophets and stones those who are sent to her! How often I wanted to gather your children together, as a hen gathers her chicks under her wings, but you were not willing!
>
> See! Your house is left to you desolate;
>
> for I say to you, you shall see Me no more till you say, 'Blessed is He who comes in the name of the Lord!'"
>
> Matthew 23:37-39

The Church is spiritually desolate because it has killed the prophetic dimension of Christ in the midst and has rejected those apostolic people sent to it with the Lord's message. This attitude and activity has destroyed the willingness of the Church to be gathered. It has not been prepared for the gathering unto the Lord.

It will not be until the Church can return to the position occupied in Psalm 118, as the people entered through the gates with the great shout of proclamation, that it will be allowed to see the Lord. The Church must once again say *"Blessed is he who comes in the name of the Lord."*

There is more here than simply a looking unto the return of Jesus Christ for the Church. The word "see" in verse 39 is *"oida"* and it carries the meaning of the fullness of knowledge coming by means of a deep perception. "Going through the gates" then becomes the position taken by the people of God of receiving and accepting apostolic and prophetic impartation; releasing a bold declaration as a result of that impartation, and coming to a place of full and complete knowing of the Lord through deep perception of Him. We must go through the gates with the great proclamation to fresh Kingdom positions in this Reformation.

The Church must be a *"righteous nation"* in the day it cries for the gates to be opened:

> In that day this song will be sung in the land of Judah: "We have a strong city; God will appoint salvation for walls and bulwarks.
>
> Open the gates, that the righteous nation which keeps the truth may enter in."
>
> Isaiah 26:1,2

The day in which this song will be sung is a day of Reformation. It is a day in which the people of God have thrown off weakness and have emerged as a *"strong city"*. It is a day when the Lord is mounting an offensive against the death-veil cast by the enemy over the mentalities of all nations and is mobilizing to destroy death forever:

> And He will destroy on this mountain the surface of the covering cast over all people, and the veil that is spread over all nations.
>
> He will swallow up death forever, and the Lord GOD will wipe away tears from all faces; the rebuke of His people He will take away from all the earth; for the LORD has spoken.
>
> Isaiah 25:7,8

A key activating principle to this thrust through the gates into the ultimate purposes of God in the nations is that the righteous nation must keep the truth. To keep is to watch, guard or protect. A new emphasis for the core truths of biblical positions must come to a Reformation people and this must be guarded against all intrusions of the enemy.

### • *Strategy Two: Prepare the way for the people.*

Note that this is not the Elijah dimension of preparing the way for the Lord as in *Isaiah 40:3-5*. Here we prepare the way for the people and this is a clear Reformation strategy for breakthrough in our time. The command in *Isaiah 61:9* connects with a flow of Reformation truth in *Isaiah 57:14*.

> And one shall say, "Heap it up! Heap it up! Prepare the way, take the stumbling block out of the way of My people."
>
> Isaiah 57:14

The way to remove the stumbling blocks out of the way of the people is by elevating the level or raising the standard. This is appropriate activity in the day of Reformation. *"One shall say"*: there must be a prophetic declaration of the design and establishment of new levels of spiritual activity in the midst of a progressive people. The prophetic announcement is a vital technology for the preparation of the way of the people. One dimension of the meaning of the word *"prepare"* is "to turn towards a completely new direction". Let us examine the internal technology of that prophetic declaration that turns the people to new things in the day of Reformation.

> "Cry aloud, spare not; *lift up your voice like a trumpet;* tell My people their transgression, and the house of Jacob their sins."
>
> Isaiah 58:1

The prophetic voice must be lifted up like a trumpet. This is key to enforcing heart change in a Reformation season. The trumpet is a consistent metaphor in the prophetic dimension and carries many applications of meaning. Let us look at some "trumpet principles".

## Trumpet Principle 1:  Access and Activation

**"You shall set bounds for the people all around, saying, 'Take heed to yourselves that you do not go up to the mountain or touch its base.  Whoever touches the mountain shall surely be put to death.**

**'Not a hand shall touch him, but he shall surely be stoned or shot with an arrow; whether man or beast, he shall not live.'  *When the trumpet sounds long, they shall come near* the mountain."**

**And when the blast of the trumpet sounded long and became louder and louder, Moses spoke, *and God answered him by voice.***

**Exodus 19:12,13,19**

God came down upon Sinai that day in all His glory. The people were forbidden on pain of death to even touch the base of the mountain, so severe was the dimension of the Spirit that fell upon Sinai.  It was only when the trumpet sounded that they could begin to approach the presence of God.  The issue here is the issue of access. The sound of the trumpet signaled that the people had access beyond the limiting regulations of God.

The trumpet also is a metaphor for the activation of dialogue between earth and heaven.  When the trumpet became louder or in the spiritual application, when the prophetic declaration in the earth became more intense, clear and profound, Moses began to speak and God answered him by a discernible voice.  The prophetic sound that is within the Church as we approach the third millenium is indeed becoming a long and loud blast, and is initiating new levels of communication with the purposes of God in heaven.  The voice of God is no longer muted; His purposes are shining clearly in the earth and a Reformation people have access today to "divine language" that they can easily understand.

## *Trumpet Principle 2: Liberty and Restoration*

"'Then you shall cause the trumpet of the Jubilee to sound on the tenth day of the seventh month; on the Day of Atonement you shall make the trumpet to sound throughout all your land.

And you shall consecrate the fiftieth year, and proclaim liberty throughout all the land to all its inhabitants. It shall be a Jubilee for you; and each of you shall return to his possession, and each of you shall return to his family.'"

Leviticus 25:9,10

The trumpet of the Jubilee, the acceptable year of the Lord *(Isaiah 61:2)*, was to sound "throughout all the land". There was no place that was exempt from the announcement that a time of liberation and release from imposition had come to the people. Thus the trumpet was associated with liberty. All who were dispossessed and alienated returned to the fullness of the original inheritance. The trumpet produced a return to a state of divine order in the midst of Israel and regulated the society out of chaos and crisis back to the accuracy of the divine plan. Family possessions were returned and past failures erased, as debtors were released from their obligations and all oppressions and injustices were brought under the correcting government of God.

There is powerful prophetic application here, as the trumpet of the announcement of Reformation in the earth begins to erase the oppressions of Pharisee spirits and religious mentalities, and returns the saints to the original power and biblical intent of God's purposes for the Church in the earth.

## *Trumpet Principle 3: Responsibility and Accuracy*

"Son of man, speak to the children of your people, and say to them: 'When I bring the sword upon a land,

and the people of the land take a man from their territory and make him their watchman,

　　when he sees the sword coming upon the land, if
he blows the trumpet and warns the people,

　　then whoever hears the sound of the trumpet and
does not take warning, if the sword comes and takes
him away, his blood shall be on his own head.

　　He heard the sound of the trumpet, but did not
take warning; his blood shall be upon himself. But he
who takes warning will save his life."'

Ezekiel 33:2-5

　　Here the watchman represents those set by the Lord
as discerners and announcers of the conditions coming
upon the Church. The watchman has the ability to see
the coming crisis; he can see "the sword". The key life or
death issue in the midst of the crisis is the sound of the
trumpet and the quality of the response to it.

　　If the trumpet was ignored and destruction occurred
then the disobedient bore responsibility for his actions.
The man who took warning saved his own life. Thus the
trumpet, or the prophetic announcement, has the ability
to provoke accurate activity in the time of crisis.

　　Those lifting up a prophetic declaration of the season of change in the day of Reformation, must be aware
that the quality and accuracy of their announcement will
either save or destroy lives. They must both "see" and
"blow". They must hear a word from the mouth of God
and warn the people *(Ezekiel 33:7)*.

## • Strategy Three: Build up the highway

　　To walk on the highway is to go forward in the
accuracy of the purposes of God. To depart from the
highway and to walk on the path is to miss the will of
God and to enter into destruction:

84

"Because My people have forgotten Me, they have burned incense to worthless idols. And they have caused themselves to stumble in their ways, from the ancient paths, to walk in pathways and not on a highway,

to make their land desolate and a perpetual hissing; everyone who passes by it will be astonished and shake his head.

I will scatter them as with an east wind before the enemy; I will show them the back and not the face in the day of their calamity."

**Jeremiah 18:15-17**

If the highways are not established in the spiritual progress of a people then they stumble and their land becomes desolate. The "land" represents the totality of their possessing in the realm of the Spirit. It has implications for the establishment of divine order in their life and represents everything that they are. When the highways are abandoned people lose their strength to make war. They are "scattered before the enemy" and are divorced from the favor of God. They are exposed to His back and not His face of favor and blessing in the day of earthly crisis. Thus the people have no power to prevail in the midst of the tumult of the earth.

When the highway experience has been abandoned, it takes a certain kind of ministry with a Reformation mentality and impartation to return the Church to a highway lifestyle.

"In the days of Shamgar, son of Anath, in the days of Jael, the highways were deserted, and the travelers walked along the byways.

Village life ceased, it ceased in Israel, until I Deborah arose, arose a mother in Israel."

**Judges 5:6,7**

Deborah represents an apostolic Reformation ministry that emerges in Israel to bring order, development and strength to a broken society. The highways are deserted and the travelers walk in a deficient and diminished experience. The end result is that the corporate order, or village life, in Israel is severely compromised. Village life represents the experience of unity, of spiritual structure and of the progress to fulfillment within an orderly plan of God.

These conditions persisted until Deborah arose in Israel. The word *"arose"* carries in its meaning a dimension of hostile intent. It means a strong emergence against resistance, which demands to be valid, proven or fixed. The Reformation spirit appears in a time of weakness and carries a dimension of strength. It arises with an impartation for establishment. Other implications in the meaning of *"arose"* carry the idea of bringing forth things that are pre-determined and pre-planned. Its strength proceeds from its inevitability.

It is important to note that even in the days of Shamgar that the highways remained deserted. Shamgar himself was a mighty warrior in Israel:

> **After him was Shamgar the son of Anath, who killed six hundred men of the Philistines with an ox goad; and he also delivered Israel.**
>
> **Judges 3:31**

Shamgar represents great ministries with mighty anointings in the Church, which demonstrate powerful things from God, but nevertheless lack the Reformation capacity to effect transformation in the operating mentality of the Church. It is vital that we comprehend this. We cannot proceed to the end of the purposes of God by building a Church that is dazzled by signs and manifestations. These things are vital and important to the development of the saints and to a demonstration of the power of God, but we must release the power of Deborah impartations which can "turn the hearts of the people" and reactivate their steps to highway positions once again.

The establishment of highways represents a time of reformation and restoration:

> Thus says the LORD: "In an acceptable time I have heard You, and in the day of salvation I have helped You; I will preserve You and give You as a covenant to the people, to restore the earth, to cause them to inherit the desolate heritages;
>
> That You may say to the prisoners, 'Go forth,' to those who are in darkness, 'Show yourselves.' They shall feed along the roads, and their pastures shall be on all desolate heights.
>
> They shall neither hunger nor thirst, neither heat nor sun shall strike them; for He who has mercy on them will lead them, even by the springs of water He will guide them.
>
> I will make each of My mountains a road, and My highways shall be elevated."
>
> Isaiah 49:8-11

In the day of Reformation God wants His mountains to be established highways elevated in the land. This speaks of a new level of development in the churches spread over the earth. They shall become mountains in the Spirit and access ways for people to come to God. The issues of elevation and prominence are clearly seen.

The highway also represents the creation of a Kingdom culture in the earth in which things determined to be irreconcilable become joined in one purpose and intent. The highway is the power of God to break satanically controlled divisions and to release the power of divine joinings:

In that day there will be a highway from Egypt to Assyria, and the Assyrian will come into Egypt and the Egyptian into Assyria, and the Egyptians will serve with the Assyrians.

In that day Israel will be one of three with Egypt and Assyria — a blessing in the midst of the land,

whom the LORD of hosts shall bless, saying, "Blessed is Egypt My people, and Assyria the work of My hands, and Israel My inheritance."

Isaiah 19:23-25

The command of God to the earth in the day of Reformation is — *"Build up the highway".*

### • *Strategy Four: Take out the stones*

The removal of the stones represents the culture and preparation of God in the midst of the Church in order to maximize the producing of purpose among His people.

Now let me sing to my Well-beloved a song of my Beloved regarding His vineyard: my Well-beloved has a vineyard on a very fruitful hill.

*He dug it up and cleared out its stones,* and planted it with the choicest vine. He built a tower in its midst, and also made a winepress in it; so He expected it to bring forth good grapes, but it brought forth wild grapes.

Isaiah 5:1,2

Taking out the stones is part of an entire process. The stones are removed in order to plant with the "choicest" vine. The vine represents the most refined aspects of the purposes and will of God. In this season God wants to cause to flow through His Church, streams of His will that have never been manifested in any other generation.

At the heart of the process is an expectation of God. He is looking for "good grapes" — majestic manifestations of accuracy and demonstrations of His glory which have been preserved for this ultimate generation. The prime issue here is far more than simply a change of the conduct of ministry. A Reformation from God involves much more than an adjustment to the worship service of a local church or an amendment to the annual programs. It demands deep mentality transformation that produces penetrative insight into God's present demands for our activity in the earth.

> **And do not be conformed to this world, but be transformed by the renewing of your mind, that you may prove what is that good and acceptable and perfect will of God.**
>
> **Romans 12:2**

It is in the transformation of the mind and in the renovation of spiritual mentality that we receive the ability to clearly see into the progressive aspects of the will of God.

We must allow ourselves to be cultured by the operations of the Spirit in the day of Reformation. We must give God access to the deepest places in our hearts if ever we will stand to speak with the tongue of the learned:

> **"The Lord GOD has given Me the tongue of the learned, that I should know how to speak a word in season to him who is weary. He awakens Me morning by morning, He awakens My ear to hear as the learned.**
>
> **The Lord GOD has opened My ear; and I was not rebellious, nor did I turn away."**
>
> **Isaiah 50:4,5**

## • *Strategy Five: Lift up a standard*

God wants to use the entire Reformation Church as a prophetic banner to the nations, showing them His true nature, love and sovereignty in the earth:

> "And in that day there shall be a Root of Jesse, who shall stand as a banner to the people; for the Gentiles shall seek Him, and His resting place shall be glorious."
>
> It shall come to pass in that day that the LORD shall set His hand again the second time to recover the remnant of His people who are left, from Assyria and Egypt, from Pathros and Cush, from Elam and Shinar, from Hamath and the islands of the sea.
>
> He will set up a banner for the nations....
>
> Isaiah 11:10-12

The Root of Jesse is both a prophetic representation of Christ Himself and the end-time Church manifesting a mighty Davidic rulership spirit and mentality in the earth. The nations will not be drawn to religion, but will be attracted to an accurate representation of Christ in and through His militant and obedient Church. Though the Church is the banner, the nations will seek Him.

When the banner or standard is raised, there will be a great initiative from the Lord to gather in the remnant from all the nations and from *"the four corners of the earth" (verse 12)*. The end of Reformation is a mighty testimony causing great gathering of the elect of God out of demonic bondage in the nations.

When a powerful Reformation Church is raised in the earth, it produces an impact in the demonic realms as the false authority of Lucifer is stripped and his forces begin to retreat off the front lines in human lives:

> "He shall cross over to his stronghold for fear, and his princes shall be afraid of the banner," says the LORD, whose fire is in Zion and whose furnace is in Jerusalem.
>
> Isaiah 31:9

The key is that there must be a blazing fire of new commitment in Zion, and the furnace of obedience and Reformation must burn within the Church.

# Chapter 6
# Activating Reformation

## Principles From Josiah

Josiah's grandfather was the prodigiously evil king Manasseh. He was the fourteenth of the kings of Judah and set a new standard for religious corruption and pure demonism in the land (2 Chronicles 33:1-9). He destroyed all the spiritual gains of Hezekiah who had brought a powerful reformation to Judah. Manasseh built altars to false gods all over the country and personally practiced soothsaying, witchcraft and sorcery. Under his government there was a revival of evil and spiritism. He caused his own sons to pass through the fire in the Valley of the Son of Hinnom. He even raised up an idol in the very house of God and defiled the consciences of the people of Judah and Jerusalem.

The Reformation of Hezekiah, the previous king, was characterized by internal cleansing of the house of God representing a purification of the conscience and the inner life of the people. All of this was destroyed by what was nothing less than a backlash of evil, as Manasseh led a spiritual revolt that defiled the worship of an entire society. Manasseh was eventually judged by God and humbled himself, but left a legacy of evil in the land unequalled by any other king.

93

He was succeeded by his son Amon who came to the throne when he was twenty two years old, and continued what by now had become an entrenched family tradition *(2 Chronicles 33:21-25)*. He revived the evil idols built by his father and refused to humble himself before the Lord. After two years, his own servants assassinated him in a palace coup. It is at this point that Josiah is elevated to the throne of Judah.

We must understand the context in which Josiah came to the throne in order to appreciate the immensity of his accomplishment. He inherits a legacy of evil that has lasted for fifty-seven years, and has no immediate patterns of godly excellence and governmental quality to guide him. In addition he is only eight years old when Amon is slaughtered and he becomes king. He is in the midst of a society that by now expects the family tradition to continue through Josiah, and certainly spiritual and moral life in Judah is at an all-time low point. Every conceivable factor operates against any great achievement in Josiah's reign, but the spirit of Reformation begins to silently but powerfully work in his life, as Josiah stands at the intersection point of human evil and prophetic intent from God. Before his birth a prophet has spoken:

> Then he cried out against the altar by the word of the LORD, and said, "O altar, altar! Thus says the LORD: 'Behold, a child, Josiah by name, shall be born to the house of David...' "
>
> 1 Kings 13:2

Reformation can break into any system and change the expected outcomes. It can redefine the traditions that have settled into the Church, because its power comes from the prophetic energy of God's divine will and desire, and not from the earthly energy of man's sinful and selfish ways. Three hundred years before his birth, an unnamed prophet spoke the word that would release this Reformation into the earth. The word came forth with accuracy, passion and divine force; now hundreds of years later a young boy, birthed in the midst of evil but configured according to prophetic decree, stands at the point of destiny and change.

The story of Josiah demonstrates to us the unstoppable force and momentum of a Reformation sent by God. Neither human tradition, history, religious corruption, nor any other earthly hindrance has the power to interrupt or resist an accurately birthed Reformation in the earth.

Let us now look closely at Josiah's Reformation and identify some of the vital characteristics and activities that brought change to the people of God in his day.

### • *He ventures outside his time and activates patriarchal destiny.*

**Josiah was eight years old when he became king, and he reigned thirty-one years in Jerusalem.**

**And he did what was right in the sight of the LORD, and *walked in the ways of his father David;* he did not turn aside to the right hand or to the left.**

**2 Chronicles 34:1,2**

The word "right" means in the original language *"to be straight, level or upright",* and has in its root meanings the suggestion of things being brought into order. It indicates the erection of powerful personal standards in Josiah's life. These standards would form the ground out of which the impetus for Reformation would eventually come. People that are inwardly bent and crooked cannot produce that which manifests the perfection of the order of God. It is processed people that bring forth a Reformation in the earth.

The measuring rod against which Josiah judged his life and established his personal patterns was *"the sight of God"*. He learned not to be diverted by the false voices and the false claims of the earth; he did not turn aside to the right or to the left. He developed consistency and persistence as powerful attributes of his character. He was focused on the goal he set himself in his kingdom. He would serve God in spite of expectations and the drag of a corrupted family history. There would be no excuses, no deviation and no slacking of his resolve. The perpendicular position against which he measured his own uprightness was only God.

Lacking standards of excellence, and finding no pathways into the divine intent in his immediate family and in the spiritual fathers immediately preceding him, he journeys backward to the glory days of the kingdom when David ruled in Judah with the prophetic power of God. He makes David's spiritual pathways his own. He imports into his own spirit the attitudes and graces that made David a model for all of Judah's kings. He bypasses the failure of his own generations and makes David his father and spiritual mentor, his example and inspiration.

Such are the principles of the Reformation of the 21st century and the mentality of the believers of this time. The failure of spiritual fathers must never be an excuse for our inability to bring forth the desire of God for our generation. The patriarchal promises and the patriarchal characteristics are still alive in the realms of the Spirit and ministered to us through the Word of God. The principles that activated the Josiah Reformation are as alive and potent to energize the things of God today, as they were when Josiah released them.

Accurate Reformation today must be built upon biblical patterns and not on human whim or preference. We must be upright and walk in the ways of the ancient spiritual fathers. It is God's original spiritual technology that we seek to touch. It is the original plan of God that we seek to enter and activate once again.

### • *He enters into strong hunger and desire for God.*

**For in the eighth year of his reign, while he was still young, he began to seek the God of his father David; and in the twelfth year he began to purge Judah and Jerusalem of the high places, the wooden images, the carved images, and the molded images.**

**2 Chronicles 34:3**

For four years Josiah did nothing but seek God the way David sought him. He did this while he was still young. The spiritual principle for application to the Reformation movement today is that a desire and hunger for God Himself is of a high priority in the days of Reformation. The primary activity of a true Reformation is a corporate re-connection with God through the revival of the spirit of hunger among the people.

David was a prodigious seeker of the face of God:

**O God, You are my God; early will I seek You; my soul thirsts for You; my flesh longs for You in a dry and thirsty land where there is no water.**

**So I have looked for You in the sanctuary, to see Your power and Your glory.**

**Psalm 63:1,2**

Josiah followed in these spiritual patterns with an expectation to see the power and the glory of the Lord emanating from the sanctuary.

Seeking God is not only an emotional activity. The word involves shades of meaning which include: *active study, seeking with a degree of application and carefulness, engaging in a pursuit.* This is a powerful activity in which all of the faculties are stirred up and focused on the new approach to God. It is this kind of prolonged activity that brings the young king to the place of certainty and resolve that culminates in the initiation of a purge in Judah and Jerusalem.

### • *He initiates a warfare against the religious spirit in the land.*

> They broke down the altars of the Baals in his presence, and the incense altars which were above them he cut down; and the wooden images, the carved images, and the molded images he broke in pieces, and made dust of them and scattered it on the graves of those who had sacrificed to them.

> He also burned the bones of the priests on their altars, and cleansed Judah and Jerusalem.

> And so he did in the cities of Manasseh, Ephraim, and Simeon, as far as Naphtali and all around, with axes.
>
> 2 Chronicles 34:4-6

Josiah launched a strong and sustained warfare against all the false religious emplacements throughout the land. This too is an essential process in every genuine Reformation move of God. One of the most deceptive positions established by the enemy in the minds of the people of God, is a refusal to understand that we operate in the midst of determined demonic invasions into the mentalities of the Church itself. Religious spirits do invade the spiritual structures of the Church:

> The enemy has damaged everything in the sanctuary.

> Your enemies roar in the midst of Your meeting place; they set up their banners for signs.

> They seem like men who lift up axes among the thick trees.
>
> And now they break down its carved work, all at once, with axes and hammers.
>
> They have set fire to Your sanctuary; they have defiled the dwelling place of Your name to the ground.
>
> They said in their hearts, "Let us destroy them altogether." They have burned up all the meeting places of God in the land.
>
> We do not see our signs; there is no longer any prophet; nor is there any among us who knows how long.
>
> **Psalm 74:3-9**

The enemies attempt spiritual coups in the midst of the house of God. They set up their banners for signs to establish spiritual control and manipulation of all the activity performed in the house. Their work is destructive and defiling, and no meeting place is exempt if they are able to penetrate. This vicious attack calls forth from the psalmist, a cry for the appearance of the prophets who can erect the true banners in the midst of the crisis in the Church. This is in fact a dimension of the Reformation move of God.

Josiah's brutal attack on religious corruption is not just simply one religious position warring against another. He operates in the power of prophetic accuracy:

> Then he cried out against the altar by the word of the LORD, and said, "O altar, altar! Thus says the LORD: 'Behold, a child, Josiah by name, shall be born to the house of David; and on you he shall sacrifice the priests of the high places who burn incense on you, and men's bones shall be burned on you.'"
>
> **1 Kings 13:2**

Josiah's ravage of falsehood in the land has been previously declared by the mouth of God and is the prescribed prophetic activity for his day. His violence has the authority of truth. He attacks the idolatrous positions with axes. "Axes" is *"chereb"*, which can also be translated as "sword" and is a clear prophetic application of the Word of the Lord as the sword of God in bringing judgment upon His enemies:

> **"For My sword (chereb) shall be bathed in heaven; indeed it shall come down on Edom, and on the people of My curse, for judgment."**
>
> **Isaiah 34:5**

### • *He repairs the house of the Lord.*

> **Now in the eighteenth year of his reign, when he had purged the land and the temple, he sent Shaphan the son of Azaliah, Maaseiah the governor of the city, and Joah the son of Joahaz the recorder, *to repair the house* of the LORD his God.**
>
> **2 Chronicles 34:8**

> **Then they put it in the hand of the foremen who had the oversight of the house of the LORD; and they gave it to the workmen who worked in the house of the LORD, *to repair* and restore the house.**
>
> **2 Chronicles 34:10**

It is evident that as far as Josiah was concerned the repair work should be supervised by trusted and loyal men. The men identified here were not only high officials in the leadership of the land, but were also strong supporters of the king and shared his vision for Reformation.

There are two words used here that give insight into the spiritual technology of the process taking place in the conduct of Reformation. In the first scripture the word "repair" is *"chazaq"*: *to make impenetrable, to strengthen by making resolute, to be firm, strong and prevailing, to make bold and courageous.* In the second scripture listed above the word "repair" is *"badaq": to close up the breaches, to mend up the gaps.* The combination of both words effectively describes the dynamic process of building that takes place in the Reformation.

The words describe the spectrum of the impact of a Reformation move. All of the gaps or deficiencies in the operating procedures of the Church are effectively corrected. All wounds or damages in the Church, which dilute the representation of Christ to the earth, must be sealed up. The Church must be the coherent, unified, powerful and single demonstrator of the majesty and glory of God to a dying humanity. The breaches must be closed.

The character of the Church, which has been subverted into weakness, compromise and fear by the invasions of religious and fleshly mentalities, must be redefined according to biblical standards and returned to apostolic strength. The resolve, strength, boldness and courage, which characterized the Church at its birthing on the Day of Pentecost, must be returned to the hearts of the saints. These are vital dimensions of a Reformation.

**• *He releases impartations that equip the entire Body.***

Then they *put it in the hand of the foremen* who had the oversight of the house of the LORD; and *they gave it to the workmen* who worked in the house of the LORD, to repair and restore the house.

*They gave it to the craftsmen and builders* to buy hewn stone and timber for beams, and to floor the houses which the kings of Judah had destroyed.

**2 Chronicles 34:10,11**

All of the different categories of workers mentioned here represent different dimensions of spiritual activity within the Church. The money distributed by Josiah, the pioneering voice of the Reformation, represents the heavenly resources and the developed doctrines; the pattern lifestyles, the prophetic clarity and apostolic revelation; the accurately released times and seasons of God that cause a Reformation process to go inexorably forward. There is a gravity flow to the initiation of Reformation activity. The king is the core activator of all that will take place in Judah.

The foremen are the pastors and elders who give oversight to local houses of God across the earth. The workmen are the activated saints who do the work of the Kingdom. The craftsmen and builders are the apostolic and prophetic resources that are called forth in the nations into full realization and expression, by the leaders of the Reformation whose voices are filling the earth.

For the Reformation to succeed, all sectors of the Church and thus the local assemblies must be activated with knowledge and clarity. The mature expression of a Reformation is not the lonely voice of the prophet shouting from a distant hill, but the corporate activity of the entire Church defining itself to the next level of the Kingdom.

Moses was not leading the people into an unknown and ignorant future. He was constantly giving them the Law. He was continuously bringing them into knowledge of the demands of the Lord. He was always adjusting their behavior patterns so that they could confidently access more of the ways of the Lord. He repeatedly defined to them what entrance into the Land of Promise would mean, and warned them to leave substantial understanding for their children so that the generations would not migrate backwards into servitude and ignorance again.

The "floor" of the house has to be restored. The floor represents the spiritual foundations of the Church. The "kings of Judah" have destroyed the floor of the building through wrong leadership and corrupting the patterns of the Spirit. We are entering the 21st century with one-dimensional mentalities, shallow faith and underdeveloped lifestyles. We are bound by strongholds of escapism and have eschewed the original mentalities of martyrdom. We are user-friendly and dazzled by the flashy entertainment methodology of charismatic "stars" of the Church. We have lost the ancient prophetic values and patriarchal stances of the first fathers, and so have compromised the dominating dimension of aggressive Kingdom advance.

Hewn stone, timber for large beams and flooring have to be purchased by reawakening spiritual hunger and desire. We must begin the construction by declaring the present revelation positions of the Spirit, and spiritually building new and relevant forms of local churches that can communicate effectively to a changed generation in the midst of the severe crises of the earth. The *"let's all escape to heaven"* mentalities and doctrinal structures will no longer suffice.

- *He redefines worship and yokes it to purpose.*

...Others of the Levites, *all of whom were skillful with instruments of music,*

*were over the burden bearers* and were overseers of all who did work in any kind of service. And some of the Levites were scribes, officers, and gatekeepers.

2 Chronicles 34:12,13

Josiah lifts the worship from simply a musical preamble to a clear governmental dimension in his Reformation. He links skill with the musical instruments to the lifting of burdens in the building process and the regulation and supervision of the work. This is a clear prophetic indicator of the extreme importance of music, singing and worship in the working out of the Reformation process in the Church today.

In every Reformation, music and singing was of great importance. David's radical move to establish the Tabernacle in Zion, contrary to the Law of Moses, was executed in the midst of a well-developed system of prophetic praise and worship that was conducted twenty-four hours a day *(1 Chronicles 25)*. In Nehemiah's day, the completion of the wall and the inauguration of a reformed society before the Lord were celebrated with the singing of two enormous choirs. They circled the city upon the wall, and sang so loudly that the joy of Jerusalem was heard afar off *(Nehemiah 12:27-43)*. In the Reformation of Ezra, the establishment of the foundation of the temple was accompanied by the sounds of the trumpets and the songs of the sons of Asaph.

In the journeying of the Israelites towards their eventual destiny, we come across this incredible event:

> **"From there they went to Beer, which is the well where the LORD said to Moses, "Gather the people together, and I will give them water."**

> **Then Israel sang this song: "Spring up, O well! All of you sing to it —**

> **the well the leaders sank, dug by the nation's nobles, by the (decree of the) lawgiver, with their staves." And from the wilderness they went to Mattanah,**

> **Numbers 21:16-18**

The people are becoming discouraged in the journey and their enthusiasm for progress begins to flag in the wilderness. They have spoken against the Lord and have been attacked by serpents in the Lord's swift judgment. They come to the place called Beer where God commands them to be gathered together so that he could give them water to drink. This is a stopping place for the impartation of new life, of restoration, of reformation of attitudes and re-alignment for the rest of the journey. A decree comes forth from Moses the lawgiver, and the nobles and princes of the people dig out the well in the dry wilderness, using the staves and scepters of their authority. What an effective prophetic picture of a place and time of Reformation, brought by divine decree and Kingdom order within the Body of Christ, as the discouraging wilderness is transformed into a place of regained strength.

But this governmental activity that brings life occurs in the midst of corporate singing and worship as the people sing the songs and command life to flow into their situation.

## •*He re-affirms the priority of the Word of God*

Now when they brought out the money that was brought into the house of the LORD, Hilkiah the priest found the Book of the Law of the LORD given by Moses.

Then Hilkiah answered and said to Shaphan the scribe, "I have found the Book of the Law in the house of the LORD." And Hilkiah gave the book to Shaphan.

So Shaphan carried the book to the king, bringing the king word, saying, "All that was committed to your servants they are doing.

And they have gathered the money that was found in the house of the LORD, and have delivered it into the hand of the overseers and the workmen."

Then Shaphan the scribe told the king, saying, "Hilkiah the priest has given me a book." And Shaphan read it before the king.

Thus it happened, when the king heard the words of the Law, that he tore his clothes.

**2 Chronicles 34:14-19**

The absolute core of Josiah's Reformation is the quality of the king's response to the re-appearance of the Book of the Law. Josiah's heart has produced action in the right direction, but finding the Law lifts his activity to a new level of accuracy, passion and acceptability in the eyes of God.

The Book of the Law drives him to an even further prophetic position. He sends out emissaries to Huldah the prophetess to inquire of the Lord. His level of spiritual discernment rises to the point that he is now acutely aware, that absolute obedience to the command of the Lord in the society of the righteous has not been fulfilled. That which was before unrecognized and unremarked is now a major issue in the mind and heart of the king.

The living core of every accurate Reformation move of God is a return to the unchallenged authority of the Word of God over human hearts. As in Josiah's Reformation, so too in the Reformation of the Church today, the Word of the Lord must lift us to new levels of sensitivity and accountability to the divine standards coming upon the Church.

In Nehemiah Chapter 8, the Book of the Law is brought out before the people to be read in public in the open square in front of the Water Gate. This is probably the most awesome and solemn point of this Reformation of reconstruction.

> **And Ezra opened the book in the sight of all the people, for he was standing above all the people;** *and when he opened it, all the people stood up.*

> **And Ezra blessed the LORD, the great God. Then all the people answered, "Amen, Amen!" while lifting up their hands. And they bowed their heads and worshipped the Lord with their faces to the ground.**

> **Nehemiah 8:5,6**

The involuntary, corporate act of rising in respect, fear and reverence for the Word as the scrolls were opened, captures in a way that words cannot communicate, the deep work of change that was taking place in the hearts of the people.

The hearing of the words of the Book tears the hearts of the people, bringing to them a new dimension of responsibility for their position before the Lord:

> **And Nehemiah, who was the governor, Ezra the priest and scribe, and the Levites who taught the people said to all the people, "This day is holy to the LORD your God; do not mourn nor weep."** *For all the people wept, when they heard the words of the Law.*

> **Nehemiah 8:9**

New understanding sweeps over the assembly and they lift their spiritual sacrifice to unprecedented levels not seen for many generations in Israel. Reformation causes a high level of excellence in spiritual activity to be released in the Church, as the saints move into uncharted territory in the quality of their spiritual offerings to God. The spiritual parameters of the Church are redesigned, and an entire generation begins to operate in dimensions that their forefathers have not before touched in God. The Word of God is the fire that enflames human hearts to this new level. It reasserts itself as the literal authority and speaking of God in the midst of His Church.

• *He leads the people to a new place of covenant before God.*

Then the king sent and gathered all the elders of Judah and Jerusalem.

And the king went up to the house of the LORD, with all the men of Judah and the inhabitants of Jerusalem — the priests and the Levites, and all the people, great and small. And he read in their hearing all the words of the Book of the Covenant which had been found in the house of the LORD.

Then *the king stood in his place and made a covenant* before the LORD, to follow the LORD, and to keep His commandments and His testimonies and His statutes with all his heart and all his soul, to perform the words of the covenant that were written in this book.

And *he made all who were present in Jerusalem and Benjamin take a stand.* So the inhabitants of Jerusalem did according to the covenant of God, the God of their fathers.

2 Chronicles 34:29-32

The maturity of a Reformation comes when covenant positions begin to flow downward from the leadership to the people binding hearts together in one common position. Josiah here represents the totally committed leadership of the Reformation. He is a leadership that has gone beyond questions, doubts and internal wrestling, and has emerged into the clarity of unquestioned surety and certainty concerning the required position in the Lord. He commits himself with *"all his heart and soul"* to obey and perform every purpose and command of the Lord in his day.

When leadership occupies such positions in the Body of Christ, there is released the downward force of Kingdom government, to bring the hearts of the willing Church into unprecedented positions of covenant for obedience to the divine purposes of the Lord. King Josiah makes the people take a stand for the Lord. There is the eradication of both complacency and doublemindedness. Every man is required to *"take a stand"*. All positions are made clear: fuzziness and inaccuracy of intent are swallowed up in the sharpness and clarity of precise positions of covenant reality.

The result is the complete eradication of abominations throughout the length and breadth of the land, and the impartation of such a spirit and mentality of consistency and permanence, that the people never swerve from their covenant position all the days of Josiah.

The pictures of stability, maturity, responsibility, commitment and honor emerging in a Reformation Church are all too clear. Reformation brings us to the most excellent positions of the Spirit. The level of agreement of intent between the king and his people, provide the ground upon which the Spirit of God is able to bring a higher level of purpose and execution of intent into the corporate body. The Word of God declares such spiritual positions both majestic and stately:

> There are three *things which are majestic in pace, yes, four which are stately in walk:*
>
> A lion, which is mighty among beasts and does not turn away from any;
>
> A greyhound, a male goat also, *and a king whose troops are with him.*
>
> **Proverbs 30:29-31**

The image of the king surrounded by his troops points to a dimension of agreement and concord of purpose between leadership and followers. Reformation brings coherence, unity of purpose and strength to maintain high levels of spiritual activity to the willing and eager Church.

### • *He elevates spiritual activity to unprecedented levels.*

So all the service of the LORD was prepared the same day, to keep the Passover and to offer burnt offerings on the altar of the LORD, according to the command of King Josiah.

And the children of Israel who were present kept the Passover at that time, and the Feast of Unleavened Bread for seven days.

*There had been no Passover kept in Israel like that since the days of Samuel the prophet; and none of the kings of Israel had kept such a Passover as Josiah kept,* with the priests and the Levites, all Judah and Israel who were present, and the inhabitants of Jerusalem.

2 Chronicles 35:16-18

The Passover feast was instituted by Moses on the eve of the departure of Israel from Egypt, and has been a major feature of every Reformation movement in the Old Testament, as the spirit of the people was renewed for fresh Kingdom advance. Let us identify some undying spiritual principles that can be found in the first Passover, that represent living realities in today's Reformation.

### • *Passover Principle One: The declaration of a new season.*

This month shall be your beginning of months; it shall be the first month of the year to you."

Exodus 12:2

The Passover changed the people's perception of time and the arrangement of the seasons of their life. On the day of their departure from Egypt their entire year changed; the month of their departure became a starting point for the record of their future. Forever the Passover would be associated, throughout their generations, with the beginning of new lifestyle, new destiny and new position and status with God. This principle of the Passover is enshrined in the activity of Reformation. Accurate Reformation redefines the Church's perception of its times and seasons in the earth. Reformation provides the ground and catalyst for the powerful entry of the Church to new levels of purpose that will forever change the way it exists in the earth.

### • *Passover Principle Two: Establishing the mentality of migration.*

**"'And thus you shall eat it: with a belt on your waist, your sandals on your feet, and your staff in your hand. So you shall eat it in haste. It is the LORD'S Passover.'"**

**Exodus 12:11**

On the night of the first great Passover, the entire society of Israel was required to dress for immediate travel. They were commanded to eat with haste, racing against the impending arrival of portentous events. This was the spirit and mentality of the Passover. They would soon be released to travel out on the long migration across the wilderness. It was a season of both liberation and challenge. The bitter servitude under Pharaoh was just about over; the long march into the fulfillment of patriarchal destiny was about to begin. The thrust forward from old positions of limitation into the fresh challenging positions of prophetic accomplishment is inseparable from the activity of an accurate Reformation.

Urgency destroyed the complacency of the time. This was a people looking toward a destination and ready to make a journey. We are not ready to depart from one spiritual level to another until our expectation has exited our present position. The very structure of the feast indicated that they were already psychologically outside of the limitations of Egyptian servitude, long before actual departure took place.

Our readiness to travel out to new frontiers of Kingdom advance, Church experience and lifestyle Christianity, must be captured in new mentalities of urgency, migration and in the tensioned excitement of the expectation of new things being released from God. Only then are we accurately positioned to enter into the depths of a Reformation process.

• *Passover Principle Three: The reality of the Lord's judgment.*

**"'For I will pass through the land of Egypt on that night, and will strike all the firstborn in the land of Egypt, both man and beast; and against all the gods of Egypt I will execute judgment: I am the LORD.'"**

**Exodus 12:12**

It is important that we realize that the transition from servitude to liberation, from limitation to destiny for the children of Israel was accompanied by severe judgment upon all the things that conspired to keep them in bondage. The power, strength and severity of the Lord were displayed to effect their transition and freedom. The day of Reformation is also a day of judgment and a severe time of the Lord. For the people of Reformation it was not to be a careless time. Careful steps had to be taken to avoid the sweeping judgments of the Lord in the land of Egypt.

### • *Passover Principle Four: Indicating a dwelling place of God.*

"You may not sacrifice the Passover within any of your gates which the LORD your God gives you;

but *at the place where the LORD your God chooses to make His name abide, there you shall sacrifice* the Passover at twilight, at the going down of the sun, at the time you came out of Egypt."

Deuteronomy 16:5,6

The Passover, as it later developed among the people of God, could not be sacrificed at any arbitrarily chosen city in the land, but could only occur at the place particularly chosen by the Lord where He established His name. The principle here to be applied in the context of the present Reformation is clear.

The place of the Passover is the place of the current unfolding of the truth of God in the earth or what Peter calls *"the present truth"(2 Peter 1:12)*. Today the place where God chooses to "make His name" is the place of the Present Reformation of the Church. It is here that we activate all of the complex principles and technologies of the Passover as we determine to move forward into the fullness of Reformation.

### • *Ancient Patterns and Extravagant Sacrifice.*

Josiah, in the midst of his Reformation, took the Passover to unprecedented heights of significance. He recovered the ancient patterns of excellence displayed by the patriarchs who advanced the affairs of the Kingdom in their day. He reconnected, in the relative modernity of his time, with the spirit of ancient Reformation. Not since the days of Samuel was such a Passover celebrated.

The fact of the matter is that there is no evidence given in the Bible that Samuel actually kept the Passover. But certainly God recognized the power and strength of a Passover celebration in the spiritual accuracy with which Samuel led Israel out of the chaos and error of the day of Eli the corrupt priest. Not since Samuel's inspired prophetic leadership provided the bridge to take Israel out of the day of the judges and into the season of the kings, had a leader arisen to express again the same mighty power of leadership in times of transition.

Josiah surpassed all the kings that went before him. He lifted Israel to the level of extravagant sacrifice and established new standards of offerings before God. Reformation is the establishing of new standards for entire generations. A Reformation redefines the quality of spiritual offerings to new levels and defines a new norm for interaction with God.

In keeping with the principles of Josiah, we must push this generation to new frontiers of faith, manifestation of the purposes of the Lord, prophetic accuracy, apostolic might and personal commitment. We must surpass the "kings" that went before us and produce the most excellent generation of purpose that both the world and the domain of darkness have ever encountered. We must touch ancient realities in our modern time and bring glory to the throne of God.

## Chapter Seven

# The Power of a Reformation: Breaking the Crisis, Blessing the Nations

In the Book of Amos, conditions are described which are prophetically very similar to the present conditions of the earth. It is a season of economic prosperity but social and moral decay. God calls Amos to be His spokesman to the nations and to Judah and Israel two years before the earthquake (Amos 1:1). Disaster is looming over the nations, but the hearts of the people are hardened to God. It is a time for Reformation; and as God calls forth the prophetic voice, He begins to undertake an inventory of the character and souls of the nations to identify the prevailing deficiencies of the earth.

## The Nature of the Crisis

The inventory is undertaken with a blast of power and from a position of supreme strength:

**And he said:** *"The LORD roars from Zion,* **and utters His voice from Jerusalem; the pastures of the shepherds mourn, and the top of Carmel withers."**

**Amos 1:2**

The nations are analyzed by the Lord and are all found to have serious defects.

• *Damascus will be judged because it has exercised oppression and undue force and dominion on its neighbors:*

> ...because they have threshed Gilead with implements of iron.

> ...I will send a fire into the house of Hazael, which shall devour the palaces of Ben-Hadad.
>
> Amos 1:3,4

• *Gaza will be destroyed because she bought and sold whole communities to the Edomites:*

> Thus saith the LORD; For three transgressions of Gaza, and for four, I will not turn away the punishment thereof; because they carried away captive the whole captivity, to deliver them up to Edom:
>
> Amos 1:6

• *Tyre will be consumed because she broke the covenants of brotherhood and merchandised her kinsmen:*

> Thus says the LORD: "For three transgressions of Tyre, and for four, I will not turn away its punishment, because they delivered up the whole captivity to Edom, and did not remember the covenant of brotherhood."
>
> Amos 1:9

• *Edom raged against his brother in tribal war and "ethnic cleansing" and incurred the judgment of God:*

> Thus says the LORD: "For three transgressions of Edom, and for four, I will not turn away its punishment, because he pursued his brother with the sword, and cast off all pity; his anger tore perpetually, and he kept his wrath forever."
>
> Amos 1:11

• *The Ammonites engaged in political warfare for territorial expansion crushing all innocent human life in the process:*

> Thus says the LORD: "For three transgressions of the people of Ammon, and for four, I will not turn away its punishment, because they ripped open the women with child in Gilead, that they might enlarge their territory."
>
> Amos 1:13

• *Moab denied the king of Edom an honorable death and disrespected the entire nation by burning the bones of its king:*

> This is what the LORD says: "For three sins of Moab, even for four, I will not turn back [my wrath]. Because he burned, as if to lime, the bones of Edom's king,"
>
> Amos 2:1

The incisive inventory continues to include Judah and Israel, who themselves are condemned along with the heathen nations. They fall into the same plane of divine condemnation. Their lists of iniquities are many and diverse:

- they have despised the law of the Lord
- their lies lead them astray
- they sell the righteous for silver
- they pant after the dust of the earth
- they pervert the way of the humble
- they lie down by every altar
- they drink the wine of the condemned in the house of their false god

*(Amos 2:4-8)*

The tragedy of the situation is that God can find no discernible difference between the nations and His people.

Incursions of the desires and cultures of the surrounding nations have obliterated the standards of Judah and Israel. As a result they have lost their special position of favor with God and fall under His judgment.

## The Compromised Church: "Reclining at the Banquet"

The conditions that we see in Judah and Israel prophetically point to the nature of the spiritual destruction in a compromised Church. These are the conditions that prevail on the eve of the release of a Reformation from God. There is a severe loss of spiritual power and a stripping of the dignity of ministry:

> **"Behold, I am weighed down by you, as a cart full of sheaves is weighed down.**
>
> **Therefore flight shall perish from the swift, the strong shall not strengthen his power, nor shall the mighty deliver himself.**
>
> **He shall not stand who handles the bow; the swift of foot shall not escape, nor shall he who rides a horse deliver himself.**
>
> ***The most courageous men of might shall flee naked in that day,*** **says the LORD.**
>
> Amos 2:13-16

It is not that the Church has ceased to perform spiritual activity. There is great activity taking place fulfilling the outward form of accurate worship, but this activity is despised by the Lord because it lacks the inner core of truth and justice:

> **"I hate, I despise your feast days, and I do not savor your sacred assemblies.**
>
> **Though you offer Me burnt offerings and your grain offerings, I will not accept them, nor will I regard your fattened peace offerings.**

118

Take away from Me the noise of your songs, for I will not hear the melody of your stringed instruments.

*But let justice run down like water, and righteousness like a mighty stream."*

Amos 5:21-24

Complacency has weakened the core of the strength of the Church in the nations. The people are at ease in Zion, trusting in dimensions of the flesh and not in the Spirit. They postpone considerations of the nearness of the Lord's judgment; enter into praise that is self-indulgent and satisfying to the flesh and soul; pervert worship into entertainment and have not grieved in their heart for the "Joseph" people of the Church who are in "affliction". They recline at the banquet and have lost the sense of Reformation urgency:

*Woe to you who are at ease in Zion,* and trust in Mount Samaria, notable persons in the chief nation, to whom the house of Israel comes!

Woe to you who put far off the day of doom, who cause the seat of violence to come near;

who lie on beds of ivory, stretch out on your couches, eat lambs from the flock and calves from the midst of the stall;

who sing idly to the sound of stringed instruments, and invent for yourselves musical instruments like David;

who drink wine from bowls, and anoint yourselves with the best ointments, but are not grieved for the affliction of Joseph.

Therefore they shall now go captive as the first of the captives, and *those who recline at the banquet shall be removed.*

Amos 6:1,3-7

# Prepare To Meet Your God, O Israel!

In spite of the conditions that have prevailed in the Church the people have not returned to the Lord. *Amos 4:6-11* details several of those negative conditions which have left the people unmoved.

*The lack of revelation in the Word:*

**"I gave you empty stomachs in every city and lack of bread in every town, yet you have not returned to me," declares the LORD.**

**Amos 4:6 (NIV)**

Deficiency in the ministration of the Word of God and a scarcity of revelation and the breaking of the seals of the Word did not provoke a spiritual hunger in the people. They remain unmoved in the midst of the famine.

*The incidence of scattered revival:*

**"I also withheld rain from you when the harvest was still three months away. I sent rain on one town, but withheld it from another. One field had rain; another had none and dried up.**

**People staggered from town to town for water but did not get enough to drink, yet you have not returned to me," declares the LORD.**

**Amos 4:7,8 (NIV)**

In the season when the rain was needed to accelerate the purposes of God to the ultimate finish, there were only scattered showers. Rain represents the revivals sent from heaven that fall only on some parts of the earth and not on others. Some areas have abundance and others are perishing for lack of the downpour of God. The people chase the revivals across the length and breadth of the earth and yet do not have enough to bring in the harvest. In spite of this, there is no cry for a global outpouring and for a Reformation storm from the Lord.

*The reality of collapsing ministries:*

**"Many times I struck your gardens and vineyards, I struck them with blight and mildew. Locusts devoured your fig and olive trees, yet you have not returned to me," declares the LORD.**

**Amos 4:9 (NIV)**

The gardens of the Lord are the ministries that cultivate Kingdom purposes in the earth. The fruit has been devoured by satanic elements and their productivity destroyed. In spite of the collapse and barrenness of ministries, there has been no cry from the Church for maturity and productivity of the Kingdom in the earth.

*The perversion of corrupted lifestyle:*

**"I sent plagues among you as I did to Egypt. I killed your young men with the sword, along with your captured horses. *I filled your nostrils with the stench of your camps, yet you have not returned to me,*" declares the LORD.**

**Amos 4:10 (NIV)**

Young men are being killed with the sword: great potential for effective ministry is being wiped out of the Church. The corruption of ecclesiastical forms is like a stench in the camp as anointed men of God return to the wearing of gowns and miters. They practice the kissing of rings, brandishing so-called "keys of the kingdom", shepherds" staffs and brass swords, associating spiritual authority with robes and the application of titles of ecclesiastical authority. Such are the plagues in the day of compromise and yet there is no cry for Reformation unto the Lord.

The cry from God is: "Seek Me and live!" *(Amos 5:5,6)* Reformation returns the focus onto God and takes the people out of the lesser forms of corrupted worship. God emerges in Israel in the midst of the establishment of standards in the camp of His people. He stands "on a wall made with a plumb line, with a plumb line in His hand." *(Amos 7:7)* Perpendicular standards will be applied to the house of Israel, and God determines to brings things back into divine order. God unveils the master-plan for the restoration of the house in the latter days. The command that comes from heaven is: "Prepare to meet your God, O Israel" *(Amos 4:12)*.

# The Re-building of the Tabernacle of David

"On that day *I will raise up* the tabernacle of David, which has fallen down, and *repair its damages;* I will raise up its ruins, and *rebuild it as in the days of old;*

That they may possess the remnant of Edom, and all the Gentiles who are called by My name," says the LORD who does this thing.

**Amos 9:11,12**

The rebuilding of the Tabernacle of David is God's strategic plan for the final empowerment of the Church in the time of the last days. By this action he will redress the imbalances, invigorate the Church and extend its borders to the nations of the earth.

There are several things to be noted here concerning the re-establishment of the Tabernacle of David. "Raise up" is *"quwm"(Hebrew): to arise with strength, to come on the scene with vigor and become powerful, to be fixed, valid and proven, to persist.* The word carries an implication of meaning that something that was once functional is to be made functional again. The concept of the Tabernacle certainly includes a definite functionality coming back to the Church. It releases a clear ability to get the job done by a removal of the paralysis that has gripped the people of God in the nations, because of seasons of compromise and inaccurate religious activity.

The emphasis in Amos on the repair work in the Tabernacle does indicate that powerful forces have devastated that which was once useful and strong. The repair will take place in the environment of spiritual resistance, but the breaches will be closed up. It will involve a coming together in the Church of things that have been ripped apart; the healing of broken mentalities and the integrating of tattered attitudes. The construction of the spiritual Tabernacle within the Church in the last days of Reformation, is a vast initiative of the Spirit in drawing together into coherence those things relevant to the plan and purpose of God, which have been separated and made impotent by years of satanic invasion and abuse.

The mandate is to repair it to the standards that pertained "in the days of old". The rebuilding of the Tabernacle will release the substantial and profound understandings of ancient time to break into the frivolous, modern mentalities of our day. We are recovering and going beyond ancient positions of the Spirit. The end result of this building thrust is for the nations to be recovered.

The first Tabernacle built by David contained no such emphasis. He simply built a place where people could worship God. David operated in a radical revelation as he constructed, within the Mosaic system, a concrete expression of a revelation dimension that exceeded the limited revelation of the Law. He did not break the Law; he superseded the Law. Yet even David did not reach to the ultimate places of understanding that Amos unfolds in this prophetic word.

We are taking the technology even further than David could conceptualize it. There was hidden truth built into the Tabernacle that was first constructed under the initiation and direction of the Spirit, even in the days of David, that has laid dormant until the time of this present Reformation. In our day of Davidic power, we are exploding past these former spiritual patterns into even greater dimensions of revelation and application of spiritual technology. The effective operation and presentation of the Kingdom combines that which is ancient and valuable because of its antiquity, with that which is new and valuable because of the freshness of its manifestation:

> **Then He said to them, "Therefore every scribe instructed concerning the kingdom of heaven is like a householder who brings out of his treasure things new and old."**
>
> **Matthew 13:52**

It is the emergence of ancient values and standards contained within our modern prophetic and apostolic thrust as we unfold the revelation of the Tabernacle, that makes this present Reformation a lethal advance of the Spirit.

Thus the Tabernacle of David with its Ark of the Covenant becomes a concrete symbol of the thrust towards Reformation. As in David's day, it represents the vast technology of the Spirit to change an entire society, and the ability to elevate human mentality to more advanced positions in its day. Ordinary men in David's day, found themselves operating in spiritual principles that exceeded the activity and spiritual levels of the Aaronic priests. So too in our day, as we bring whole communities within the Church into the experience of the Tabernacle, men will be lifted to as yet unforeseen levels of spiritual potency and relevance to the will of God.

Let us identify some principles that were activated in David's day as he led Israel up to the heights of Reformation in his time. These principles provide a bedrock foundation for the replication of Davidic Reformation activity in our time.

# Four Principles for the Tabernacle

• *Tabernacle Principle One: The Ark was brought up after a new level of kingly presence was established over all Israel.*

Then all Israel came together to David at Hebron, saying, "Indeed we are your bone and your flesh.

Also, in time past, even when Saul was king, you were the one who led Israel out and brought them in; and the LORD your God said to you, 'You shall shepherd My people Israel, and be ruler over My people Israel.'"

Therefore all the elders of Israel came to the king at Hebron, and David made a covenant with them at Hebron before the LORD. Then they anointed David king over Israel, according to the word of the LORD by Samuel.

1 Chronicles 11:1-3

All these men of war, who could keep ranks, came to Hebron with a loyal heart, to make David king over all Israel; and all the rest of Israel were of one mind to make David king.

1 Chronicles 12:38

*The mobilization of men of high quality:*

There has never before nor since been seen in the community of Israel such a mobilization of men of high quality. These are the men who have been through the forming process with David in the cave of Adullam and have emerged out of the Ziklag situation. They are men of great discerning and great warfaring ability. Long before David manifested the victory and the prevailing favor of the Lord in his kingdom, these men had discerned the activity of the Lord upon his life. They came to him long before manifestation; they were pioneers of perception of the changing order of the times; they could see in the Spirit where the future density of the Lord's anointing would rest. They came out of the old order of the kingdom which was passing away. They were of the tribe of Benjamin, the brothers of Saul.

> **Now these were *the men who came to David at Ziklag while he was still a fugitive from Saul* the son of Kish; and they were among the mighty men, helpers in the war,**
>
> **armed with bows, using both the right hand and the left in hurling stones and shooting arrows with the bow. *They were of Benjamin, Saul's brethren.***

> **1 Chronicles 12:1,2**

In every Reformation such men of might emerge, having their genesis in the order that is passing away, but with a vision planted in the future things of God in the earth. These are men of transition, who are willing to abandon the old even while the new is yet not totally formed and has not yet emerged into full power. They are the strong pioneers of transition.

*The reality of divine order and the recognition of spiritual measure.*

The warriors who came to David possessed awesome anointings and spiritual abilities. They were accurate in their resolve and fulfilled prophetic declarations over the life of the king *(1 Chronicles 11:10)*. There were individuals among them who had performed far greater exploits than even David had. The least of them was over a hundred and the greatest was over a thousand *(1 Chronicles 12:14)*. They could make war in conditions that were adverse to war. They had crossed Jordan in the times of flood, surprised the enemies and had defeated them *(1 Chronicles 12:15)*. Yet these were men who could keep rank and walked within their respective measures of ability and calling without breaking out into rebellion and disorder.

The environment of Reformation is one in which the magnificent strength of individual anointings is contained within the divine order of God. Such conditions must prevail if God is to reclaim control of the advance of the Kingdom in the earth, and accurately direct the Church in a single global operation to the attainment of the finish of all things. In the 21$^{st}$ century we cannot afford the breaking of the ranks, as wayward ministries, driven by philosophies of their own advance and prosperity, struggle outside the divine order of God to elevate themselves. There must be a vast operation of the heart throughout all the territories of the global Church, as God sanctifies the aims and objectives of His servants by the moving of His Spirit in the days of Reformation.

Control does not come from a single "papal" authority, committee or council. We are not a religious organization; we are the Church of Jesus Christ. Control comes through the coherent operations of the Spirit through the vastness of the Church in the earth as men come into divine order, recognizing the ranking order of the Kingdom and the set limitations of their own ability, strength and measure.

*The recognition of true spiritual leadership in the Church:*

The anointing of David at Hebron, was preceded by the coming together of the separated houses of Israel and Judah. The move that culminated in the bringing back of the Ark of the Covenant and the establishment of the Tabernacle of David, derived its strength from the achievement of community unity under the leadership of David. There is an anointing that propels David to

the heights of his purpose in God, that can only be activated by the voice of a coherent community, even
though David had received a prophetic anointing
administered by Samuel when the horn of oil was
poured out upon him *(1 Samuel 16:12,13).*

There are two important dimensions to this anointing at Hebron. Firstly the elders of Israel recognize
David as the fulfillment of God's prophetic plan. Saul
had been the choice of a people locked into a natural and
earth-influenced mentality. Their demand for and choice
of a king did not line up with the prophetic plan of God.
It is accomplished in the midst of prophetic displeasure
and is a sign of their rejection of the plans and purposes
of the Lord:

> **Then all the elders of Israel gathered together and
> came to Samuel at Ramah**
>
> **and said to him, "Look, you are old, and your sons
> do not walk in your ways. *Now make us a king to
> judge us like all the nations."***
>
> **But *the thing displeased Samuel* when they said,
> "Give us a king to judge us." So Samuel prayed to the
> LORD.**
>
> **And the LORD said to Samuel, "Heed the voice of
> the people in all that they say to you; for they have not
> rejected you, but *they have rejected Me, that I should not
> reign over them.***
>
> **1 Samuel 8:4-7**

In their choice of David, the elders rehearse the
prophetic charge given to Samuel by God to be spoken
over the young man David on the day of his first anointing *(1 Samuel 16:1-3).* This indicates that the people are
once again the custodians of the prophetic record spoken
over them in times past by the great prophets. They
have departed from the selfish desire to be like the other

nations in having a king of their own choosing, and are being governed again by the command of God.

Secondly, the people identify the location of genuine spiritual leadership and authority within the camp of God:

> "Also, in time past, *even when Saul was king, you were the one who led Israel out and brought them in;* and the LORD your God said to you, 'You shall shepherd My people Israel, and be ruler over My people Israel.'"
>
> 1 Chronicles 11:2

The people are at last able to discern clearly between religious position and operations, and valid spiritual authority and effectiveness. They recognize that even though Saul exercised the manifest power of kingship and administration over the people of God, that he was not the one who moved the people deep into the accurate purposes of God.

This perception is the beginning of a valid Reformation. Reformation is not a religious hype or a new spiritual fad with a shelf life no longer than the interest of the people. Reformation that engineers new levels of spiritual revelation and expression is led by men who can actually lead Israel out and bring them in. They are the designers of the journeys of the tribes who operate under direct authority from God.

In this next season of the Church, the people of God must come to a higher level of discernment, that would enable them to identify those apostolic leaders across the world, in every territory and sector of the global Church, who carry the effective word for this Reformation. Cultural pride, racial preferences, traditional patterns and organizational constraints, which have sharply limited the manifestation of the true shapes of the Church must be abandoned, as the elders of Israel abandoned their limitations. The Davids of the earth must be received by the Church and the advance to Tabernacle positions must now begin!

• *Tabernacle Principle Two: The Tabernacle required the establishment of a new stronghold.*

> And David and all Israel went to Jerusalem, which is Jebus, where the Jebusites were, the inhabitants of the land.
>
> Then the inhabitants of Jebus said to David, "You shall not come in here." Nevertheless *David took the stronghold of Zion* (that is, the City of David).
>
> 1 Chronicles 11:4,5

*Finding a new epicenter:*

The process toward the establishment of the Tabernacle involved finding a new epicenter. An epicenter is a stronghold of mentalities, position and understandings out of which we operate, that enables us to bring forth the things of God that are relevant to the time. It is a place from which mighty deeds can occur. For David, the movement was from Ziklag to Zion. Ziklag represents the personal stronghold of David:

> Now these *were the men who came to David at Ziklag* while he was still a fugitive from Saul the son of Kish; and they were among the mighty men, helpers in the war,
>
> 1 Chronicles 12:1

> *Some Gadites joined David at the stronghold in the wilderness,* mighty men of valor, men trained for battle, who could handle shield and spear, whose faces were like the faces of lions, and were as swift as gazelles on the mountains:
>
> 1 Chronicles 12:8

It was the beginning of his strength and the place of mobilization of his army while he was a fugitive during the days of Saul, before the Reformation occurred in the land of Israel. When David is elevated to the throne of all Israel he moves to a new stronghold. Zion is the stronghold of God. It is the place of God's strength and the place of the demonstration of God's power:

> **For the LORD has chosen Zion; he has desired it for His dwelling place:**
>
> **Psalm 132:13**

The Reformation process is a movement in the Church out from our own personal strongholds to the strongholds of God. We must move out of the places where our own personal strength is guaranteed and our own ministry activity is powerful within our own spheres, into a dimension where the strength is entirely of God. The Zion position is the place where God dwells; it is a place of the mighty demonstration of kingly power, a place that is forever associated with the glory of God.

*Driving out the Jebusites:*

God's stronghold of Zion is established in the teeth of opposition from the lame and the blind:

> **And the king and his men went to Jerusalem against the Jebusites, the inhabitants of the land, who spoke to David, saying, *"You shall not come in here; but the blind and the lame will repel you,"* thinking, "David cannot come in here."**
>
> **Nevertheless David took the stronghold of Zion (that is, the City of David).**
>
> **Now David said on that day, "Whoever climbs up by way of the water shaft and defeats *the Jebusites (the lame and the blind, who are hated by David's soul)*, he**

**shall be chief and captain." Therefore they say, "The
blind and the lame shall not come into the house."**

**2 Samuel 5:6-8**

The soul of the Reformer must hate the Jebusite
principle in the Church. The Jebusites represent that
which corrupts the place that will be the stronghold of
God. It is important that we note that the city of
Jerusalem, which represents the place of the future
expression of the glory of God, was once named the city
of Jebus, the place occupied by the Jebusites who resisted
the entrance of the newly crowned David to the position
of power. Jebus later became the place at which the
Tabernacle was established. If the Tabernacle of David
is to be rebuilt and established in our day as Amos
prophesied, then we must destroy the Jebusite principle
in our own times.

It is the lame and the blind that will repel the
advance of the Davidic spirit to a place of Reformation:
this is the strong core of the Jebusite mentality. The
"lame" represent all the things that prevent us from
walking strongly in the purposes of God. The "blind"
represent all of the factors that destroy our discernment,
perception and revelation of the intent and desires of
God for our day. The combination of the blind and the
lame produce a Church locked in the iron grip of religion
and programmed activity, that can never access the Zion
positions of accuracy in the purposes of God and the
explosion of His will in this planet. Reformation exter-
minates the Jebusites from the hill of the Lord.

It is through the activity and sovereign working of
the Holy Spirit in the hearts of men in the day of Reformation that these cruel enemies are destroyed. David's
battle for Zion was not a frontal military assault but a
guerilla advance by unconventional means up to the
Jebusite stronghold:

**Nevertheless David took the stronghold of Zion (that is, the City of David).**

**Now David said on that day, *"Whoever climbs up by way of the water shaft and defeats the Jebusites* (the lame and the blind, who are hated by David's soul), he shall be chief and captain." *Therefore they say, "The blind and the lame shall not come into the house."***

**2 Samuel 5:7,8**

His mighty men climbed up into the tower by the way of the watershaft, which indicates the activity of the Holy Spirit. The result was the establishment of a house from which the blind and the lame were forever barred. It became a proverb for the Davidic era. From that time the people said: *"The blind and the lame shall not come into the house."*

Such is the house of Reformation that Amos promises will be rebuilt as God brings the end-time Church to a place of power in the earth. It is a place from which all the factors that repel the advance of the purposeful power of God are entirely banished, until it becomes a commonly possessed realization among the people of God, that the blind and the lame must never enter the house of God. Zion represents the acquisition of mentalities among the community of the faithful that are totally welded to the advance of the will of God in our time.

*Living in the stronghold:*

**Then *David dwelt in the stronghold,* and called it the City of David. And David built all around from the Millo and inward.**

**So David went on and became great, and the LORD God of hosts was with him.**

**2 Samuel 5:9,10**

The Church must begin to live in the stronghold of God and begin to exhibit a "stronghold lifestyle" to the nations of the earth. With the Jebusites exterminated David renamed the place and called it "The City of David". The lifestyle associated with the stronghold of Zion became forever associated with the name of David. The manifestation of God and the lifestyle of David became one and the same: the City of David became the Hill of the Lord.

Not only did David occupy the stronghold but he began to strengthen his position there and build fortifications to assure occupation for many generations. He built all around and then inward until Zion was fortified both within and without. This is such an expressive picture of the mentality of the Church in the day of Reformation. We must build externally in a fresh and new demonstration of God's power and strength in an accurate, revelatory 21$^{st}$ century lifestyle that will impact the nations. But we must also build inwardly and create divine strongholds within, in unbreakable mentalities and spiritual characteristics that will cause Kingdom power to be expressed from us in clarity and purity in the days ahead.

Our future greatness depends on the acquisition of these values. David was always a mighty warrior, prophet and a leader of men. He inspired confidence, loyalty and ignited the hearts of all who came near to him. But it was only after he ascended to the Zion fortress position, drove out the Jebusites and built in the stronghold, that greatness was added to him by God Himself:

> So David went on and became great, and the LORD God of hosts was with him.
>
> 2 Samuel 5:10

The greatness of the Church in the future is the greatness of God in the earth. Through the processes of Reformation, our fame and our name will always be one and the same with God's fame and God's name in the nations. Jesus Christ effectively sits upon the throne of David: we cannot be separated from the rulership and power of our Lord.

• *Tabernacle Principle Three: The Tabernacle involves a desire to bless the nations.*

Then David consulted with the captains of thousands and hundreds, and with every leader.

And David said to all the assembly of Israel, "If it seems good to you, and if it is of the LORD our God, let us send out to our brethren everywhere who are left in all the land of Israel, and with them to the priests and Levites who are in their cities and their commonlands, that they may gather together to us;

and let us bring the ark of our God back to us, *for we have not inquired at it* since the days of Saul."

Then all the assembly said that they would do so, *for the thing was right in the eyes of all the people.*

**1 Chronicles 13:1-4**

*Removing selfish concerns:*

David's first desire to return the Ark to Israel was primarily concerned with the well-being of his own nation. His first movement to Reformation was based on the democratic principle of what seemed right in the eyes of all the people. Thus the corporate motivation to Reformation was built upon the lowest common denominator available — the general approval of the people based on self-centered concerns.

This initial thrust into a Reformation position is destroyed by the hand of God. In the midst of the march towards Jerusalem, God kills Uzzah as he tries to steady the falling Ark *(2 Samuel 6:5-7)*. The Ark of the Covenant, which represents the very core of the activated Tabernacle of David, was placed in the house of Obed-Edom the Gittite for the period of three months.

*Blessing the Edomites:*

Obed-Edom is a significant character in the decoding of the meaning of the Tabernacle as it applies to our current situation. His name means "the son of Edom". The name first appears in the context of Esau's despising of the patriarchal birthright and the covenants of the Lord to the seed of Abraham (Genesis 25:30). Throughout the scripture and in the record of the history of the nation of Israel, the Edomites were the enemies of the people of God and maintained a perpetual hatred through their generations. They refused the Israelites passage through their territory in the days of the great migration out of bondage under Pharaoh (Numbers 20:18-21). The Edomites, under the direction of Hadad, were the greatest adversaries of King Solomon. They made alliances with Pharaoh and Hadad even married the sister of the Egyptian Queen Tahpenes (1 Kings 11:14-25). During the bitter destruction of Jerusalem in the reign of the Babylonian King Nebuchadnezzar, the Edomites participated in the plunder and agreed to the destruction of Jerusalem (Psalm 137:7).

In the historical record during the days of the Macabees in the inter-testamental period, the Edomites were subjugated and incorporated into the Jewish nation as the province of Idumea but continued in hatred and bitter hostility. When Jerusalem was attacked by Titus in 70A.D., 20,000 Idumeans were released into the city and terrorized it with violence, robbery and pillage during that terrible season of destruction. In the military campaign of Amaziah against the Edomite people of Seir, we are told that the Edomites were a nation of idol worshippers *(2 Chronicles 25:14)*.

Such is the heritage that Obed-Edom represents. In addition he is a Gittite or identified with the chief Philistine city of Gath, the dwelling place of Goliath the major adversary of Israel in the early days of David's emergence into spiritual significance. Obed-Edom spiritually represents a principle that is eternally hostile and set in hatred against the things of God and the people of God, but yet the Ark is placed in his house. The spiritual and revelational implications are both remarkable and inescapable. This is a clear indication of the heart of God to send His presence and blessings to the nations that in their operations and position are hostile to the rule and the presence of the Lord.

David has a change of heart, attitude and orientation when he sees that the presence of the Ark in Obed-Edom's house brings a definite blessing of the Lord to the whole household:

> **The ark of the LORD remained in the house of Obed-Edom the Gittite three months. And the LORD blessed Obed-Edom and all his household.**
>
> **Now *it was told King David, saying, "The LORD has blessed the house of Obed-Edom and all that belongs to him, because of the ark of God."* So David went and brought up the ark of God from the house of Obed-Edom to the City of David with gladness.**
>
> **2 Samuel 6:11,12**

We must recognize that the Ark of God or the presence of the Lord blesses the nations; it redeems the Edomites. This is the prophetic promise of Amos to be fulfilled in the day that the Tabernacle of David is spiritually rebuilt and repaired among the people of God. All the nations and all the remnant of Edom who are ordained to be brought into the family of faith will be reclaimed by a rampant Davidic Church.

We struggle toward operational perfection in the day of Reformation, not primarily to effect a personal escape from this earth, but to provide a powerful redemptive pathway for the nations. The mentality of the Church has been occupied by the desire for personal escape. We have taught the "Rapture" until it has produced an escape mentality, and has become a stumbling block to dominant mentalities of Kingdom advance and the development of mighty compassion for the multitudes held in the grip of destructive satanic forces *(Matthew 9:35-38)*. Now in the season of Reformation, while continuing to look upward for the imminent return of the Lord, we reach out with new strength to the unfortunate prisoners of the earth. We do this by constructing powerful Reformation positions within the global Church that will impact the nations for their own blessing from the Lord.

• *Tabernacle Principle Four: The Tabernacle demands a prescribed mentality.*

So they brought the ark of God, and set it in the midst of the tabernacle that David had erected for it. Then they offered burnt offerings and peace offerings before God.
                                                          1 Chronicles 16:1

And on that day David first delivered this psalm into the hand of Asaph and his brethren, to thank the LORD:

Oh, give thanks to the LORD! Call upon His name; make known His deeds among the peoples!

Sing to Him, sing psalms to Him; talk of all His wondrous works!
                                                          1 Chronicles 16:7-9

The Tabernacle could really be called David's Tent over the people. Inside the Tabernacle a revolution was taking place. Moses' Law was still in force over the people of Israel. There had been no general indication through the prophets that the season of Law had been changed by God, but yet David was able to elevate the entire society, by the power of his revelation, to a higher level of operation and experience in the things of the Spirit. The Tabernacle of David invalidated the restrictions of Moses' Tabernacle over the mentality of the people.

The worship established by David in the Tabernacle was really the activating feature of the operation. It created a culture and an environment in which the people experienced spiritual freedom from the limitation of the Law. In other words there was a prescribed mentality within the full functionality of the Tabernacle of David. There was a powerful prophetic dimension to the Tabernacle which proceeded in great proclamation of His glory, His wonders and His deeds among the nations of the earth *(1 Chronicles 16:8-10, 23-24)*. The psalm delivered by David into the hands of Asaph established in the operations of the Tabernacle accurate patterns for future activity. But it also imparted the mentality, revelation stance and spirit of David to the people, as they came forward into the presence of God in the atmosphere of Davidic praise and worship. The patterns of the worship emphasized the remembering of the covenant promises of God and the certain promise that the Lord will come to judge the earth *(1 Chronicles 16:33)*.

All of these factors point to essential things that form part of the rebuilding of the Tabernacle of David in our day of Reformation, as God reaches out to possess those in the nations called by His name. There is a prescribed mentality in the day of Reformation. Just as David deliberately designed and imparted the powerful spirit of prophetic proclamation, covenant affirmation and agreement with the purposes of the Lord, so too in our season for the Reformation to be activated and become effective in the earth, we must enter the prescribed mentality of the time.

The nations will not be impacted by the old tired mentality, attitude and spirit of the Church. David in establishing the Tabernacle constructed an entirely anti-Mosaic mentality and practice, and he put systems in place to ensure that it was consistently produced. The mentality of Reformation cuts across the prevailing systems of thought of the time. It introduces the saints into a dimension of the Spirit that allows them to advance further into the realms of God than the prevailing patterns allow them; just as David's people came before the Ark into positions allowed only to the high priest under the Mosaic system.

As Amos prophesied, the Tabernacle will be rebuilt by God in our day. The global Church will come into new radical mentalities and release purposes of the Lord far in advance of the expectations of our generation. There will be new levels of covenant-making in the Church, as a new leadership emerges to direct the 21st century believers into the depths of the purposes of the Lord. Reformation re-activates the spiritual journey of the Church in a strong and definite way. We will proceed up to Zion positions, casting out the "lame" and the "blind" that resist and hinder the accurate release of the will and mind of the Lord in the earth. As Davidic positions and mentalities become the generally accepted possessions of the Church, we will reach out to the nations in a new and more powerful way, impacting them with the manifestation of the glory of the Lord and bringing the blessing of the Lord to those who are called by His Name.

## Chapter 8

# A Generation for Reformation

## Transmitting Across the Generations

God's purpose is never limited to one generation only. He is the God of Abraham, Isaac and of Jacob. His purposes cross over into the generation to come and can never come to maturity except they carry the seed of generational transference or trans-generational impartation. The word generation refers to a period of time in human history that is characterized by a quality, a condition or a class of men. In speaking of a spiritual Reformation in the Church and in the earth we are speaking of generations on a deeper level than simply in chronological terms. A Reformation creates a new spiritual generation in the global Church because it shifts the operational strength, the revelation parameters and the general identity of a whole people. It creates a new quality, condition or "class" of men in the earth, and so is actively preparing a generation to carry the torch of the advance of the Kingdom to a new level.

Part of the definition of the greatness of the Lord is that His praise or the knowledge of His greatness is communicated from generation to generation:

> **Great is the LORD, and greatly to be praised; and His greatness is unsearchable.**

> One generation shall praise Your works to another,
> and shall declare Your mighty acts.
>
> Psalm 145:3,4

God does things in the midst of His people, and reveals His intent in prophetic dimensions to the generation of fathers so that these things would not be hidden, but revealed to the next generation. Things hidden from ancient time must be revealed. That is the dynamic process of building a spiritual generation in the earth and causing the progressive revelation of the majesty of God to be consistent and strong:

> I will open my mouth in a parable; *I will utter dark sayings of old,*
>
> which we have heard and known, and our fathers have told us.
>
> We will not hide them from their children, telling to the generation to come the praises of the LORD, and His strength and His wonderful works that He has done.
>
> For He established a testimony in Jacob, and appointed a law in Israel, which He commanded our fathers, that they should make them known to their children;
>
> *that the generation to come might know them, the children who would be born, that they may arise and declare them to their children,*
>
> *that they may set their hope in God,* and not forget the works of God, but keep His commandments;
>
> Psalm 78:2-7

The end result is that the dynamic transfer of the testimony of God consistently happens from generation to generation, causing the recipient generation to "arise and declare" the things that they have heard. Each spiritual generation must be stronger and more declarative than the one preceding it. The testimony must grow stronger; more hidden things must be brought to light as the generation sets its hope in God.

What is communicated is the strength and the power of God. These are the divine characteristics that primarily define the generation of transition. These words define in general terms the qualities that are carried over when a spiritual generation comes to "grayheadedness", has exhausted its deposit of life and God is about to shift to another level in the Spirit:

> Now also when I am old and grayheaded, O God, do not forsake me, until I declare *Your strength* to this generation, *your power* to everyone who is to come.
> **Psalm 71:18**

"Strength": *zerowa (Hebrew):* refers to the raw ability of innate power and also is used in the Bible to refer to the strength of military forces. It focuses on the transmission of the revelation of the absolute power and "military" might of God to cause a continuing impact to be made in the next generation. Therefore the transitional generation of a Reformation goes out in a clear revelation of the mighty power of God. "Power": *gebuwrah (Hebrew):* can be translated mighty doings or deeds that are accomplished in an explosive display of wisdom or accuracy in the spirit. It is a capability that is directed by perception; a power that is seasoned with counsel. These are the attributes that are released to the generation of Reformation.

Psalm 48 speaks of the Zion positions of the Church in the earth and the entire psalm thrusts towards the reality that these mighty revelations of Zion must be transmitted to the generation that follows. It is not a fuzzy revelation that is declared, but a clear and precise definition of the shapes and features of what God wants to establish in the earth:

> Walk about Zion, and go all around her. Count her towers;
>
> Mark well her bulwarks; consider her palaces; that you may tell it to the generation following.
>
> Psalm 48:12,13

What is declared to be the possession of the generation of transition is that which we have received by walking about, going all around, counting, marking well and considering. It is the product of this deliberate acquisition of revelation that is imparted to the generation following.

The things that we have examined above define once more the nature and prevailing characteristics of the Reformation generation. It is a generation that receives a carefully transmitted and fully declared revelation of the force and power of God. It is a generation of structure, clarity, experience and prophetic ability to exceed the activities of its spiritual fathers and to cause the glory of God to manifest in the earth in an unprecedented way. Let us now consider some of the active principles and characteristics that apply in a generation in the very midst of a current transition to Reformation positions.

## Identifying a Generation of Reformation

The Word of God is filled with incidences of entire societies shifting from one dimension of life to another. Joshua led the survivors of the Exodus across the Jordan River into a new state of life. Nomads became city dwellers and occupied lands taken by force of arms from the idolatrous people who previously owned them. The corrupt order of Eli gave way to the prophetic priesthood of the judge Samuel and renewed the authority of

God in the nation of Israel. The long painful shift from the Saul era to the Davidic era brought the nation into a fresh prophetic dimension, and set the stage for the emergence of the glorious kingdom of Solomon and the construction of the Temple. Kings like Josiah brought Reformation to the land, as he obliterated the errors of his fathers and built new platforms of faith and service in the hearts of the people.

The generation that lived at the time of Moses was a Reformation generation that actually lived through the practical shift from the bondage under Pharaoh, to the liberty of the long march through the wilderness to a new life with God. More than any other chapter, Exodus Chapter 12 captures the moment of transition and takes us into the technology of that awesome night, in which all of their prayers throughout the days of servitude become crystallized into the moment of deliverance and change.

Let us look at several conditions that pertain to the generation living in the day of Reformation:

## • *Condition 1: Advancing in the crisis.*

And it came to pass *at midnight that the LORD struck* all the firstborn in the land of Egypt, from the firstborn of Pharaoh who sat on his throne to the first-born of the captive who was in the dungeon, and all the firstborn of livestock.

So Pharaoh rose in the night, he, all his servants, and all the Egyptians; and there was a great cry in Egypt, *for there was not a house where there was not one dead.*
**Exodus 12:29,30**

Reformation is the product of a system in turmoil in which man has lost his way. It defines a system in which we can no longer stay. However we must be able to interpret the crisis in which we live. Turmoil is not a reason for despair or depression but is a signal that God has initiated the process of change.

When God sent Moses in to speak to Pharaoh, God promised to harden the heart of the king of Egypt so that His wonders might be demonstrated to the stubborn king:

"You shall speak all that I command you. And Aaron your brother shall speak to Pharaoh, to send the children of Israel out of his land.

*And I will harden Pharaoh's heart, and multiply My signs and My wonders in the land of Egypt.*

But Pharaoh will not heed you, so that I may lay My hand on Egypt and bring My armies and My people, the children of Israel, out of the land of Egypt by great judgments.

*And the Egyptians shall know that I am the LORD,* when I stretch out My hand on Egypt and bring out the children of Israel from among them."

**Exodus 7:2-5**

There would be no transition without the season of utter crisis. Behind the crisis was the unfolding purpose of God. It was the national turmoil that would break through the obscurity in the mentalities of the people of Pharaoh and show them the awesome power of God. Reformation meant not only liberation and advancement for the people of God, but also a statement of divine power and the clear recognition of God among the nations. The same principle exists today in this present season of the empowering of the Church.

Midnight represents the day of crisis and the season of change. It is the moment of the Lord's action; the

hour in which all the prophetic promises come into actualization, and years of prayer distil into precise activity
both in heaven and here on the earth. The generation
whose accurate advance begins in the midst of the crisis
of the times is the generation of the future. The midnight horror in Egypt was the birthing of this new people and was the signal from heaven that the time of their
advance had come.

### • *Condition 2: Sacrifice for corporate wholeness.*

"Speak to all the congregation of Israel, saying:
'On the tenth day of this month every man shall take
for himself a lamb, according to the house of his father,
a lamb for a household.

Your lamb shall be without blemish, a male of the
first year. You may take it from the sheep or from the
goats.

Now you shall keep it until the fourteenth day of
the same month. *Then the whole assembly of the congregation of Israel shall kill it at twilight.'"*

**Exodus 12:3,5,6**

A sense of sacrifice must arise in the dying hours of
the old dispensation as the Reformation generation pre-
pares for the actuality of transition. It was emphasized
to the Israelites that the lamb must be killed at twilight
as the light of the day faded out of the sky.

When Joshua was preparing the second generation
for the invasion of the land of Canaan, he led them
through the passage of Passover at twilight on the plains
of Jericho *(Joshua 5:10)*. They had just been circumcised
and separated from the reproach of Egypt and were con-
fronting great military campaigns ahead. The manna
would soon stop falling from heaven and they would
have to eat of the food of the land of conquest. For them,
as it was for their fathers before them, the twilight sacrifice marked the passage to a new dimension of life.

The corporate activity of the entire community bound them together in a sense of common mission: *"The whole assembly must kill it."* The implication is of the multitude of individual household sacrifices in Egypt in that darkening hour, being accounted as one great corporate sacrifice by God. In this season of Reformation there must be a sense of sacrifice rising in the heart of the body of Christ. We must be willing to be spiritually discomfited and be ready to pay the price for a day of migration to new positions. This must be accomplished, not in the mentality of fracture, but in the spirit of oneness and integration as the experience and challenge of change binds us together in a new way.

### • *Condition 3: Emphasis on personal purity.*

**"So you shall observe the Feast of Unleavened Bread, for on this same day I will have brought your armies out of the land of Egypt. Therefore you shall observe this day throughout your generations as an everlasting ordinance.**

**In the first month, on the fourteenth day of the month at evening, you shall eat unleavened bread, until the twenty-first day of the month at evening.**

**For seven days *no leaven shall be found in your houses,* since whoever eats what is leavened, that same person shall be cut off from the congregation of Israel, whether he is a stranger or a native of the land.'"**

**Exodus 12:17-19**

The command from God through Moses was: *Remove the leaven from your houses!* If anyone was found eating leaven he was to be cut off from the congregation of Israel. Leaven invalidated the journey.

The scripture itself provides us with its own interpretation of what this spiritually represents. Leaven points to characteristics of inward corruption which God will not tolerate or draw near to. It points not only to the corruption of religious mentalities and Pharisee practices *(Matthew 16:6)*, but also to the operations of the old nature from a past state which must not be allowed to enter and pollute the new experience:

> **Your glorying is not good. Do you not know that a little leaven leavens the whole lump?**
>
> **Therefore purge out the old leaven, that you may be a new lump, since you truly are unleavened. For indeed Christ, our Passover, was sacrificed for us.**
>
> **Therefore let us keep the feast, not with old leaven, nor with the leaven of malice and wickedness, but with the unleavened bread of sincerity and truth.**
>
> **1 Corinthians 5:6-8**

The leaven principle is that the corruption inevitably spreads, and the new experience will be overtaken by the patterns of the old if a critical separation from those patterns does not take place. The old leaven must be purged and must not be allowed to enter into the feast. Paul points to the critical area of internal attitude and transparency of presentation before God. Unleavened bread represents a heart filled with sincerity and truth.

• *Condition 4: A lifestyle of immunity from the crisis.*

> **"And you shall take a bunch of hyssop, dip it in the blood that is in the basin, and strike the lintel and the two doorposts with the blood that is in the basin.** *And none of you shall go out of the door of his house until morning.*
>
> **For the LORD will pass through to strike the Egyptians; and when He sees the blood on the lintel and on the two doorposts,** *the LORD will pass over the*

> *door and not allow the destroyer* to come into your houses to strike you."
> **Exodus 12:22,23**

The season of transition is the time of the active presence of the destroyer. There were two entirely different patterns of reality occurring in Egypt that night. The Lord was passing through to strike the Egyptians, but at the same time He was *"passing over"* the generation of transition who were coming out. There was a divine restraint upon any destructive activity upon the houses of the Israelites. The Lord would "not allow" the destroyer to come in.

This is a tremendous spiritual metaphor that captures the complex patterns of life in the day of Reformation. The Church is coming out of bondage, urged onward by the dynamic working power of the Lord. For the people of God it is a season of safety in the midst of the storm, as they are kept separate from the prevailing crisis by his restraining power.

The key to the survival of the people of God is that they must not go out of the door of their houses until the break of day. They must abide under the set conditions of their safety. The blood on the lintel is the mark that they are protected, and identifies the people that are entering the passage to Reformation and change.

It is the mark of Reformation that we carry today that ensures that we prevail in the midst of the crisis on the earth. Jesus Himself spoke of the necessity to enter into a mentality and behavioral position that was oppositional to the prevailing attitudes of the earth in the last day:

> And you will hear of wars and rumors of wars. See that you are not troubled; for all these things must come to pass, but the end is not yet.
> **Matthew 24:6**

The crisis will come, but we must ensure that we do not participate in the frantic traumas of the earth. The people of Reformation enter biblical positions in the day of the earth's crisis, just as the children of Israel entered under the mark of the blood and so came out of the crisis in Egypt triumphant and free.

### • *Condition 5: Vigilance in the season of change.*

**It is a night of solemn observance to the LORD for bringing them out of the land of Egypt. This is that night of the LORD, a solemn observance for all the children of Israel throughout their generations.**

**Exodus 12:42**

The word used here translated "solemn observance" is *"shimmur"(Hebrew): a vigil, to stay awake through the night.* Spiritual alertness is required in the season of Reformation and all the factors that cause us to lose our watchfulness must be removed from us. All aspects of cultural bondage, yokes of philosophy, dead tradition and binding religious mentalities and positions have to be stripped away, leaving us sensitive and alert to the commands coming from heaven for the final mobilization of the Church.

## On That Very Same Day...

Thus the Passover captures within it specific conditions that identify a generation that has come to the place of readiness to make the critical shift to a new position in the unfolding purposes of the Lord. The Passover demanded intense personal involvement. No foreigner could eat of it unless he was first circumcised and become as a native of the land. No uncircumcised person was allowed to participate in the remembrance of that great night of breakthrough in Egypt *(Exodus 12:43-51)*. No one could stand afar off and enter into the process of the Passover. To exit from Egypt you had to buy into the experience and participate in the journey.

For four hundred and thirty years the cries of the people went up to God until the fullness of the time determined by prophetic decree had come. There arrived a clear, shining moment when heaven touched the earth, and in one day the liberation from Egypt to a new order of life came powerfully in:

> And it came to pass at the end of the four hundred and thirty years — *on that very same day* — *it came to pass* that all the armies of the LORD went out from the land of Egypt.
>
> **Exodus 12:41**

Such are the conditions of our Present Reformation.

The clear, clarion cry for Reformation has been issued in heaven and has been heard in the earth by the prophetic ear of the Church. The proclamation of the new advance is being issued in every quarter of the global Church and the Spirit is stirring the battalions of the Reformation people into action. This is a season of destiny unmatched by any other. It is a day of great exploits, of majestic migration to the next level in God and of Kingdom breakthroughs. It is a Day of Reformation!

**COME LORD JESUS!**